"Alternately creepy and captivating, drawing readers in with the same you-can't-not-look quality of a highway crash . . . there will be some stiffs who just can't get past Booker's subject. Readers who do will find that her story is only partly about dead people. It's the living ones that make the book."

—Associated Press

"A darkly comic memoir of life and death in urban America."
—*Booklist* (starred review)

"Filled with both tragedy and humor and wholly compelling in its humanity." —*Publishers Weekly*

"Booker's descriptions of her experiences of loss, dating, and coming-of-age are interesting, but it's her revelations about the daily workings of a funeral home in a poor urban setting that are transfixing." —*The New York Times Book Review*

"[Booker's] knack for detail, character descriptions, dialogue, and exposé of personal indiscretions make for a gritty, moving, and often funny read. . . . Her insider's story manages to uplift and turn a glimpse of the dark side into a bright reveal of humanity." —*Creative Loafing*

"Fascinating. . . . The perspective that Booker gained from her years dressing bodies is rare and valuable. She has cultivated a soft compassion and a hard sense of gallows humor, which, when correctly combined, can create great literature and a powerful sense of humanity." —*City Paper* (Baltimore)

"Booker beautifully captures her years as a mortician's right-hand woman in her new memoir *Nine Years Under*, taking readers behind the scenes, explaining in vivid prose what happens in a place people only visit when they don't want to be there. . . . Ultimately, the book is a love story to a community, to an unsung yet heroic small business, and to her adopted family, particularly patriarch Albert Wylie, conduit to the great beyond."   —Biographile.com

"Looking for something with a great plot? Something different, delightful, but a little dark? Then you need *Nine Years Under*. . . . This is a wonderful, wonderful book that sounds squirmy yet is anything but. So grab *Nine Years Under*, because if you think you'll like it, you're dead right."   —Marco Eagle

"In this knockout first effort, Booker colors in the lines of the victims of gang violence, the innocents who catch a stray bullet, and the guilty who leave behind heartbroken family."
                                                           —*Essence*

"In *Nine Years Under*, Booker poetically infiltrates the private world of black funeral home culture. The book serves as a magic intersection of this mysterious mortuary milieu, the black church, and middle-class black Baltimore to spin a story that Booker is uniquely positioned to set to prose. You will laugh and cry, be horrified and hopeful. But at the end of a dark ride through valleys of suppressed emotion, every reader will realize that at the end of the darkest and most violent of rainless thunder storms, our own tears can set up rainbows of promise."
                                         —Jeff Johnson, author of
                          Everything I'm Not Made Me Everything I Am

"*Nine Years Under* is a sparkling debut—brimming with love and bursting with life. Booker's Baltimore is equal parts *The Wire* and *The Cosby Show*. She doesn't shrink from the realities of life in an inner-city funeral home, but she is also a loving witness, documenting the big-hearted community that takes care of its own. Told with compassion, wit, and good old-fashioned storytelling, Sheri Booker gives us unforgettable characters who will make you laugh right up until they break your heart."   —Tayari Jones, author of *Silver Sparrow*

"In *Nine Years Under*, Sheri Booker has accomplished quite a feat. She somehow was able to bring a tremendous amount of light and life to a story about the strange and often dark business of death. For that, I applaud her."

—Jason Reynolds, coauthor of
My Name Is Jason. Mine Too.

"You've never read a book like *Nine Years Under*. I fell in love with Sheri, a plucky and nervy teenager who took a risk that changed her life. Through love, laughter, and tears, Sheri takes you to a world many of us will never experience. And she does it with lively writing, awesome characters, and a sharp sense of humor. Who knew the world of death was filled with so much life?"   —Aliya S. King, author of *Diamond Life*

ALVIN GRAY

Sheri Booker is a writer, poet, spoken-word artist, and teacher. She is the author of *One Woman, One Hustle* and has traveled the United States reciting and performing her poetry. In 2007, she lived in rural South Africa, where she taught journalism skills to African women and worked as an editorial assistant for an international literary magazine. Sheri has written for *Urbanite*, *Channel Magazine*, *The Amazwi Villager*, *A Magazine* and *East County Times*. Sheri has an MFA in creative nonfiction from Goucher College. She currently lives in Baltimore.

www.sheribooker.com

NINE YEARS UNDER

COMING OF AGE IN
AN INNER-CITY FUNERAL HOME

SHERI BOOKER

GOTHAM BOOKS

GOTHAM BOOKS
Published by the Penguin Group
Penguin Group (USA) LLC
375 Hudson Street
New York, New York 10014

USA | Canada | UK | Ireland | Australia | New Zealand | India | South Africa | China

penguin.com
A Penguin Random House Company

Previously published as a Gotham Books hardcover

First trade paperback printing, July 2014

2 4 6 8 10 9 7 5 3

Gotham Books and the skyscraper logo are trademarks of Penguin Group (USA) LLC

The Library of Congress has catalogued the hardcover edition of this book as follows:
Booker, Sheri, author.
Nine years under : coming of age in an inner-city funeral home / Sheri Booker.
p. cm.
ISBN 978-1-59240-712-5 (hardback) 978-1-59240-762-0 (paperback)
1. Undertakers and undertaking—Maryland—Baltimore.   2. Albert P. Wylie Funeral Home
(Baltimore, Md.)—Employees.   I. Title.
HD9999.U53U5217 2013
338.4'73637509752—dc23
2012049711

Printed in the United States of America
Set in Bembo • Designed by Spring Hoteling

For my mother, my hero and best friend

"A human isn't fully mature until they've had to grapple with death, and neither is a culture."

TOURÉ

CHAPTER
ONE

THE custodian who controlled the thermostat for Baltimore's summer heat was a smug son of a bitch—relentlessly unleashing lethal doses of sweltering humidity and dampness into the inner-city air. There was no way to dilute the blazing mixture.

Fired up like an open rotisserie, it roasted the skins of innocent bystanders—gravediggers, policemen, and outdoor merchants—until they were a golden-brown delight. Those who could tolerate the unbearable heat were desperate for any sort of hydration—a fire hydrant, a frosted bottle of water from a street vendor—or for God to at least have enough mercy on the city to let it rain.

I had stopped petitioning the heavens for miracles four days before, when my aunt Mary's light went dark. My mother discovered her slumped figure just in time to see it gasping for its last taste of oxygen. We were now en route to see her remains for the first time since she was taken from me, and in just a few moments, I would be standing inside a building designed to transition corpses from lifeless organisms into living memories.

None of us should have been surprised, but eight wide eyes stared at Great-Great-Aunt Mary's unresponsive body that horrible night. My parents, my sister, and I hovered around the bed where she lay slouched in an eternal slumber, her eyes shut tight and her body completely still. My father knew CPR; he was a policeman. And my sister had been certified in CPR for the camp where she worked that summer. But no one moved. As I stood there, the plush carpet shifted like sand beneath my bare toes and the walls of the room felt like they were closing in on me.

My home had felt foreign for weeks. The hospice nurse stacked the shelves with medical equipment, a few weeks' supply of Depend adult diapers, morphine patches, bandages, and gauze. People were in and out all the time: nurses, visitors, and ministers back-to-back. If Aunt Mary had been in her right mind, she would have called it "signifying or meddling in her business," but she hadn't been coherent for a while.

We watched her shrivel and shrink as the cancer consumed most of her body. The hospice nurse warned me to savor every moment because time was running out. She gave me a purple double-pocketed folder with booklets about preparing for death and what to do when your loved one has a terminal illness, but I shoved it into a drawer after her shift was over and didn't look at it until weeks after the funeral when we were cleaning out Aunt Mary's room. Neither flowery folders with colorful brochures nor compassionate nurses can prepare you for the inevitable.

After weeks of hospice care and enough meds to tranquilize an army, Aunt Mary slipped through our fingers like twenty thousand dollars on a gambler's bad day. No little girl wants to stand by and witness her hero surrender. I wish someone had told me back then that hospice care was the beginning of the end. Then I wouldn't have blamed myself for not doing enough. I wouldn't have felt ignored by God.

•   •   •   •

I imagine Al Wylie and his son Brandon were at their kitchen table picking at a dozen well-seasoned Maryland crabs that night when the call came in. This was neither the first nor the last time they would get their hands dirty that day. It was the middle of June, just before the seasons changed shifts, the time of year when homicides and heatstrokes kept the two of them occupied. The call volume was steady and there was little time for entertaining friends, especially since they spent three or four mornings each week directing funerals and supervising burials, and most of their afternoons were busy with preparing human remains for viewing.

Later, Al and the new female apprentice he had just hired would strip down from their fancy suits into old jeans and long-sleeve shirts for a night of embalming. In the mornings, that same crab shack would be converted back into the staff cafeteria and lounge. No matter what time of day or night, one thing remained the same: Al Wylie was the boss, and the chair on the right side of the table was for him alone.

No one was ever surprised when Al's pager went off in the middle of his spontaneous crab feasts. The sound of it buzzing was far too familiar. Death was just like a debt collector: It had no respect for the day or time when it called. The sound could sizzle in his pocket at his best friend's wedding or shake the entire pew at church, but when death called, Al Wylie had to answer. He was always on call, and just like a doctor, he'd excuse himself, check in with the operator, and graciously bow out of his activity.

Without even looking down at it, he'd already know it was the answering service. When his volume of calls picked up, he'd hired a twenty-four-hour live-call center that took his calls after business hours. They were the only ones who called this late in the evening. Many times he would be fast asleep when his pager began vibrating on the dresser. A call after midnight was usually for a body in a nursing home. Unlike hospitals, most nursing homes don't have refrigeration or a morgue where the body can be placed until morning.

There are firms who hire drivers to pick up bodies during the night. But Al Wylie, whose business was just beginning to grow, didn't mind saving money and making the removal himself. Since his son Brandon had just graduated from high school that year, he always had someone to accompany him on the late-night drives if need be.

That night, I imagine him hopping out of his seat, wiping the peppery blend from his hands, and heading next door into the main office. After scrambling for a working pen and a piece of paper, he dialed the answering service.

My mother had been the caller who interrupted his dinner that night. She sat by the phone waiting for him to return her call. The telephone number for his funeral home was always listed on the back of the church bulletin, and as a result we had all subconsciously memorized it. So unlike other families, we didn't have to flip through the yellow pages or search around the house for old funeral programs that had a director's contact information. Sometimes, while my pastor preached his sermons, I would doodle the number over and over until he was finished. The number was also listed on the back of some of the stick fans at church that the ushers used to cool off the little old ladies who caught the Holy Spirit.

As the chairman of our deacon board, Al Wylie was also a respected figure in the church. We already knew we would use him for any death in our family except my mother's. She said that she didn't want him and his son looking at her naked body when she passed away. She joked that she would rather go to someone she didn't know, someone who wouldn't try to cop a feel.

In what felt like seconds, Deacon Wylie was on the line with my mother.

"Yes, mum," he uttered after each sentence my mother spoke. He and Brandon always said "ma'am" like they were from the Deep South. Had the police already been there? He needed to know before he made any further move. If the police hadn't yet released the body, coming to make the removal would be a waste of time, because he might be forced to stand around for hours while they ruled out foul play. But Aunt Mary was in hospice care, so she wasn't required to be taken to the medical examiner's office to determine the cause of death.

Wylie told my mother that he was praying for her and would be at the house within the hour. It was comforting to know that a direct intercessor with God was praying for us.

Just before dark our neighbors had retreated into their homes for the evening after enjoying the chill of an approaching summer breeze. Now the flashing lights and roar of the fire engine had summoned those who didn't have the decency to peek through their venetian blinds to view the commotion from their front porches. As a police detective, my father was used to this type of scene, but he had never been on the opposite side. He was always the one in uniform who showed up and made sure that a crime had not been committed. But this time he was the one with the big eyes, trying to keep composed.

We were all unusually calm. Not one of us had cried yet. In fact, my mother had given my sister and me directives to straighten up our already spotless home before anyone arrived. I grabbed the Pledge and began dusting our furniture while my sister did a drive-by on the living room floor with the vacuum.

My father walked the uniformed men up the stairs and into the bedroom where Aunt Mary lay lifeless. My sister and I watched from the hall as the paramedics grabbed her arm to take her pulse. They offered to try to resuscitate her motionless body, but my parents did not want to disturb God's will.

After the policemen pronounced her dead, I had a few moments alone with her. I pulled her rocking chair close to the bed and grabbed her hand. It still felt warm.

"I'm sorry," I told her. "I'm so sorry."

I felt guilty knowing how distracted by foolish things I'd been in her final weeks. A boy I was dating at school had just broken up with me and I hadn't been able to sleep or eat while we were on the outs. The truth was I'd felt like I was dying from a broken heart. Just before Aunt Mary's death I had scribbled in my journal these exact words: *I want to die.* Maybe God had confused my request.

The back door of the funeral wagon slammed shut, echoing through my deserted Northeast Baltimore neighborhood. The dim street lanterns shed just enough light to guide the gentlemen up the walkway and to my front door. Then I heard a big voice coming from my living room.

"Where she at?" Deacon Wylie asked. He followed my father through our living room and up the stairs into the room where I sat holding her hand, hoping to keep it warm. As he approached, I could hear him explaining how he and the boys were in the middle of eating crabs when his pager went off. He had left Brandon home to finish the crabs with his friends, and instead brought along another man who worked for him to help. Having Deacon Wylie there lightened the mood. Although it was very peaceful, it had begun to get heavy in the house.

That night he was not wearing one of the suave suits that he wore to church on Sundays, but slacks and a thin jacket. He still looked professional, and even as he joked, it was clear that he understood the seriousness of the matter. He started his work intently, and it was then I realized that this was definitely real.

It was all done ceremoniously. He pulled a white sheet over Aunt Mary's face and wrapped the rest of her shriveled body. Then he and his assistant gently lifted her from her hospital bed and placed her inside a body bag attached to a wobbling stretcher. They slowly zipped the black bag from foot to head until she was no longer visible, and then lifted the stretcher and maneuvered it down the staircase, cutting the corners with the precision of furniture movers. After rolling her out of the house, they placed her in the back of the funeral wagon. As I watched the station wagon drive up the street, I thought how inhumane it was to have someone who was just breathing and blinking moments ago zipped up in plastic and strapped into the back of a car.

• • • •

I was about seven years old when I experienced my first major loss. I had spent the whole afternoon at my neighbor's house playing with toys. I had taken with me the Gabby Bear—a cheaper version of Teddy Ruxpin—my grandfather had given me as a Christmas gift. Since I didn't get to see my grandfather that often, it was a toy I cherished.

Gabby had big bright blue eyes that rolled open and shut as he talked. He wore a red-and-white-striped shirt and jean shorts. His mechanical mouth told my favorite story about Willy the one-horned billy goat. I played with Gabby so much that my dad kept the jumbo pack of D batteries on his dresser.

After a few hours of play, my parents called me home for dinner. I left Gabby at my friend's because I assumed I would return later, but my parents had plans for us to visit my grandmother.

During dinner it began to rain, but we still had to go see Big Mama. When we walked outside to get in the car, my father noticed Gabby sitting on the porch, soaked from the rain. His tiny head had been partially cut off and was leaning to the side. The spongy filling poked through his neck, and the wires and tape recorder were protruding from his back. I picked up all his pieces and held him in my arms. The pain stung. I tried to press the play button just to hear his voice, but nothing happened.

So, like the police detective that he is, my father launched a full investigation. He walked over to our next-door neighbors' house and began an interrogation. My best friend told him that she'd accidentally dropped Gabby down the basement stairs. I was horrified, and the halfhearted apology she later gave me meant nothing. In my eyes, she was a murderer, but in my father's eyes I was the culprit because I hadn't taken good care of something that was mine.

So my father took me inside while everyone else waited in the car. We went up to my parents' bedroom and my father spanked me. I knew that my sister and I were disciplined that way only when my parents were trying to teach us an important lesson. It was how they had been raised by their own parents, and they continued the tradition. That's when I learned the importance of protecting the things you love. When I got in the car, Aunt Mary could sense that I had gotten in trouble, so she whispered in my ear that she would get my father later.

Yet, here I was eight years later, still unable to save something I cherished. I thought my father would be disappointed again, but it wasn't his hand that was beating me this time. It was all me.

* * * *

THE car ride to the funeral parlor was excruciating. The air conditioner in my mother's car blew hot air at us, so I had no other option but to roll down the back windows and hope that a breeze might blow through. My bone-straight hair was known to frizz into an Afro puff on hot summer days, and the lenses of my glasses could leave me in an embarrassing fog whenever I moved from the heat outside to cooler air. As beads of sweat began to form above my brow, I reached into my purse for the stack of tissues I had packed beforehand. I still hadn't cried, and it had been three whole days since Aunt Mary died. I was afraid that this might be the day I would lose my composure.

My parents had allowed me to make most of the important decisions about the funeral. I had chosen the casket and the cemetery plot; I had even written the obituary and listed myself in it twice. I had chosen the photo for the front of the program. The only thing I hadn't done was pay for it all myself.

When we finally arrived, I adjusted my dress, reapplied my clear lip balm, and sat up straight. We were a few minutes early, a direct result of my father's military discipline, so we sat in the car staring silently at the building before us. The stern look on my father's face said that it wasn't a good idea for me to have any kind of emotional display then and there.

My mother turned off her engine at exactly three P.M., and we emerged from the car dressed in our Sunday best. I usually loved being the first one to enter when we arrived anywhere, but not one of us was in a hurry to get to the front door that day. My father asked if we had everything, but there was nothing we needed. The funeral home had taken care of it all.

Mr. Wylie greeted us at the door and directed us into the room where Aunt Mary lay waiting for someone to come admire her. There in her fancy gown, flawless salt-and-pepper wig, and shiny clip-on earrings, Aunt Mary was an angelic presence that radiated throughout the room. I'd wanted her to be dressed in a brand-new Easter suit that she had never worn, but her sister insisted that she be buried in one of the shrouds from Mr. Wylie's catalogue. It reminded me of a nightgown when I first saw it, and I was totally against it, but now, seeing her in it, I realized that the pink and pearl-laced gown complemented her in every way. It also matched the grand pink-and-white casket with the custom-made sculpted angels I'd chosen. The casket cost more than a living room furniture set.

Once we approved the body, Aunt Mary would be properly unveiled to visitors and friends for the wake. But the thought of people fawning over her, dripping meaningless tears as if they were the ones who cared for her in her last hours, made my pressure drop. They hadn't been the ones to endure her morphine-induced tantrums and the vulgar words that had no business coming from the mouth of a sweet eighty-seven-year-old woman. They didn't have to deal with her random midnight babblings about Moses and her mama and her dead sister, China Baby. They hadn't been there to witness her frustrating memory lapses or to force-feed her Ensure when she pursed her lips shut and shook her head like a stubborn three-year-old. In my eyes, no one deserved to get close enough to touch her because no one had had to learn to love her the way I had.

As a smooth, sorrowful musical blend of organ and trumpets saturated the air, my parents, my sister, and I gathered around her casket, just as we had circled her deathbed. But as we quietly reminisced, I found myself obsessed with Aunt Mary's appearance.

The choppy layers of her wig needed a bit more teasing, so I reached inside my purse for a comb and began to pull the synthetic hairs apart until they fit her usual style. Her skin tone was off too. I wondered if the mortician had used a liberal hand with the makeup or if it was just that her complexion had naturally darkened. We had given Mr. Wylie her eyeglasses, along with her dentures so that her mouth would look full, and I could see that he had put the false pearly whites into her mouth but had left her glasses on the pillow beside her. Apparently, corrective lenses were an accessory you didn't need to pack for heaven.

Once I was satisfied with Aunt Mary's appearance, I reached beneath the scattered Kleenex in my purse for my camera. But before I could get one click in, my father insisted that I put it away. In his eyes, it was disrespectful to take photos of a dead person—you just had to live with the memories that were already stored in your mind. I would later inherit this same theory.

Beside her casket was a gold-lettered plaque with an electric candle and a large framed photo of her attached, a simple reminder of her beauty. Inside the open hood there was a bronze nameplate engraved with her date of birth and a dash followed by her date of death; a bouquet of flowers covered her swollen hands. The air smelled of oranges, a scent that I will always associate with death. I would later learn that the music, orange spray, nameplate, hand bouquet, and plaque were all signature touches exclusive to the Wylie Funeral Home. Much of the competition charged extra for those frills.

The viewing room was lined with cards and floral arrangements, including the bleeding heart we'd purchased—a heart-shaped combination of white carnations and red roses that stood tall on a flower stand. I thought of what Aunt Mary used to say, scornfully: *Give me my flowers while I'm living.*

As I moved toward the foot of the casket, I saw that the right side of Aunt Mary's face looked as full as a blowfish. I asked Mr. Wylie if it was the cancer that caused the swelling, but he pointed to her photo in the plaque at the head of the casket, which revealed the same lopsidedness. Compared to the picture, Aunt Mary looked like a deader version of herself.

It wasn't until that moment that I realized the woman I had known was really gone. Her body was present, but her soul was absent. For the first time in my life, I had lost something irreplaceable: a human life.

. . . .

BEFORE I experienced death, I was your typical teenage girl. I loved boys and music and talking on the telephone. My sole ambition was to make my parents proud. They'd gotten away from the rough streets of West Baltimore before crack consumed them. We lived in a nice home on the other side of town, and as a policeman and a school principal, they'd worked hard for their success. We were certainly not the Huxtables, but my parents would have done anything to make sure their girls had everything.

After Aunt Mary died, the ground beneath me shifted. I expected the world to pause for my grief—and it didn't, not even for a moment of silence. I'd always found comfort in gospel music, but those days the lyrics to Lil' Kim's album *Hard Core* blared through my earphones instead. I wanted something raw, gritty, and profane. Living in the house where Aunt Mary had died made me feel like a killer. I wanted to pour bleach on everything or set Aunt Mary's belongings on fire. I even thought about burning the clothes I had worn that night.

I didn't want to erase her memory; I just wanted to rid myself of every single reminder of that moment.

I couldn't understand how my parents were keeping it together, getting up each morning and going to work as if nothing had happened. I couldn't even get out of bed. I knew they wanted to be strong for me, but I wanted them to have that "Damn, damn, damn" moment like Florida Evans had on *Good Times*. When Florida's husband, James, died, her children couldn't understand why she was laughing, dancing, and celebrating. She insisted that she was fine, but as soon as she was left alone, she broke, throwing a dish on the ground and screaming, "Damn, damn, damn!" I wanted permission to mourn, but I never felt like I got it.

In the midst of burying Aunt Mary, the one thing that remained constant was our faithfulness to church. We were right back in there the following Sunday, so my father could get back to counting the offering with the other trustees and my mother could recruit new members for the Lord. Clearly, I was the only one that felt salty with God. And even though I loved singing as lead vocalist for the youth choir, I had decided that I would never lead a song again.

The second Sunday after Aunt Mary died, I just didn't feel like going to church. I tried to pretend not to hear my mother calling my name and to ignore the smell of my father's Sunday breakfast. But it didn't work—they got me up and forced me to go.

I sat there in the pew with my lips poked out and my arms crossed. When the minister asked us to stand for prayer, I remained seated until my mother reached over and pinched me so hard that I almost screamed. I knew better than to play with

God, and I definitely knew I shouldn't try my mother either. But I didn't care.

Right after the offering, I slipped into the hallway for a quick sip of water. I wasn't interested in my pastor's remix of a sermon I had heard before. As I walked toward the doorway that led to the main hallway, I ran smack into Deacon Albert P. Wylie. He greeted me with his usual handshake, casually bending his knees while sticking out his arm and slightly hunching his shoulder over. He didn't do it the way the other deacons did it, all stiff and serious.

"What's up, Little Booker?" He laughed. I could always count on him to put a smile on my face. It was never what he said; it was always the way he said it. His laugh was huge and revealed the silver plate in the roof of his mouth. Although he was totally gray on top, he was only fifty-one at the time and quite hip, always looking sharp in one of his custom suits. Though not the most attractive man, Mr. Wylie had swagger and attitude that could make any woman blush. His walk, like that of Sherman Hemsley's character, Deacon Ernest Frye, on the eighties hit *Amen,* was one of undiluted confidence. When he extended his hand, I could see his initials embroidered on his shirtsleeve.

A self-made man, Deacon Albert P. Wylie had held the position of chairman of the deacon board at my church for the last five years. Every time its doors opened, it was Deacon Wylie who had unlocked them. On Sunday mornings, he was there bright and early for Sunday school. Sometimes during service he would even say the morning prayer. While kneeling at the altar he would remove his glasses, and with a whiny voice of repentance he would cry out over the microphone, "Oh

Loooord, stop by here this morning, Lord. Oh Loooooord, if you listening, a few of your humble servants are here before you."

But church was also where he got a lot of his business. His latest promotional fan pictured his staff, with him dead center, sitting in a backward-turned chair with his arms hanging in front, so that you could clearly see his personalized diamond bracelet.

It felt strange seeing him in church that Sunday, knowing that he had just buried my aunt. I don't know what I was expecting him to say, maybe something that would give me closure. But he didn't mention the funeral at all, not even to ask how I was handling the loss.

"Booker, what are you doing this summer?" he asked.

"Working for you." It was a joke, but I felt foolish for even suggesting such a thing, especially since I knew he wouldn't take me seriously.

"When can you start?" He wasn't laughing.

"Tomorrow." I kept the conversation going, half kidding. If he was teasing, then I figured I'd laugh it off with him.

"Okay, come to the funeral home tomorrow."

"I'm serious," I said. I didn't know what I was saying or why I was saying it, but I couldn't back down.

"I'm serious," he said as if I had just locked myself into a verbal contract with him. He took out a calendar book to check his schedule. "Yup, we have a viewing tomorrow."

Mr. Wylie already knew I could be dependable. As a lead vocalist, I was a shining star at church, belting out hymns every second and fifth Sunday. And I was a good student. My parents made sure that my honor roll status was proclaimed each quarter during Sunday morning announcements. He knew my family, and particularly my older sister, well. She'd been president of the youth choir before she went to college, and on Sundays, Mr. Wylie would have my sister greet his foxy dates, escort them into the church, and even sit with them sometimes. When he decided to marry one of the mink-coat-wearing women, he asked my sister to be in his wedding. But he suddenly called it all off. That woman would go on to marry his friend, while he married the second Mrs. Wylie, a meek and holy woman in our church, instead. They were in the middle of a divorce when he offered me the job.

"What will I have to do?" I asked nervously, wishing I had asked these questions before I agreed to work at a funeral home.

"Just answer the door and phone. You will work the evening shift, from four to eight P.M."

"Okay." It didn't sound so bad. "Do I need to dress up?"

"Yeah, wear a dress like the one you're wearing now." He pointed to the black knee-length dress I had on.

We shook hands and sealed the deal. On my way back into the sanctuary, I prayed that my mother would insist that working in a funeral home was a bad idea.

After church, Mr. Wylie went directly to my mother to pitch the idea and asked her to bring me to the funeral home the next day. To my surprise, she didn't think twice about it, because she trusted Mr. Wylie. And so with no great formality, I answered the call to serve the dead and grieving.

For the first time in my life, I had made something happen on my own. My previous jobs had been courtesy of my mother. Two years before, when I was only thirteen years old, I had been an intern at the Maryland State Department of Education. That position got me into the White House to meet President Bill Clinton during one of his Saturday radio addresses. The summer Aunt Mary died, I was supposed to start a different internship with the local board of education, but after her death, I didn't feel up to it. Working at the funeral home would be much different, and I didn't mind shedding my good-girl image. Being hired by Mr. Wylie on the spot seemed like divine intervention. It was no accident that I didn't end up at Pretzel Time, where the rest of my girlfriends worked.

I was taught that there was one way to deal with death: Ignore it. But working with Deacon Wylie would allow me to run toward it, as I felt compelled to do. It would be like becoming a death detective. I wanted to know what had happened to Aunt Mary while she was in Deacon Wylie's care, and I also felt that being at the same funeral home would somehow keep me connected to her. It all made sense to me then.

While my mother didn't mind lending me to Deacon Wylie for a few days a week, my father wasn't too enthused about the idea. He told me to make sure that I stuck to answering the door and phone, and whatever I did, I had better not go wandering around in the basement where the embalming took place. I assured him that I had no intention of ever going to the basement. I was just there to open the door and answer the phone. That was it. That was all. Or so I thought.

CHAPTER
TWO

GRIT and grime tend to avoid the corner of Gilmor Street and Harlem Avenue, where the Albert P. Wylie Funeral Home stands shining like an opaque jewel in the rough. The brick brownstone stretches three stories high above the cellar. Dope fiends linger in the adjacent park waiting on a fix while the neighborhood drug dealers protect their territory on the opposite street corner. The fiends are sometimes rolled through the wide basement door, packaged in a body bag, after overindulging in their indiscretions. The dealers, too, have been known to send business up the block when their turf has been threatened. They press their ears to the streets in an attempt to hear the tiptoeing of the enemy so they won't find themselves stretched out in chalk on the aged concrete. In a way, both groups are providing a service to the community—a steady yet unnatural way to keep the small funeral home thriving.

On many afternoons, grieving loved ones make melodramatic entrances and storm back out of the front doors, unable to contain their overwhelming emotions. Some tip over the railing that runs beside the stairs from the door to the sidewalk, as if they wish to jump and join their loved one on the other side. Others pace up and down the street shouting obscenities. Some simply retreat to their cars, hoping to find their composure or something close to it buried in their glove compartments. Occasionally, a tissue will slip from someone's trembling hand and land on the ashy pavement. The fearless teens from the middle school across the street sometimes hide behind the front doors of the copper-toned building, attempting to steal a glance inside. No matter how they end up there, on foot or by stretcher, the funeral home is never at a loss for visitors.

Not everyone in that building is lying stiff on a ceramic table or frozen in a gigantic freezer. The other souls who have become intimate with death are living, breathing creatures whose curiosity or bloodline has led them to work in the business. For them, there is a constant cycle of life as long as there is death.

Soon I would become one of those people, an insider in a world foreign to most of humankind, a world that you can't quite prepare yourself for, a world so mysterious that you can't envision it in your dreams and can only pray to avoid in your nightmares.

• • • •

THAT first day, two weeks after Aunt Mary's funeral, I stood atop the marble staircase that led to the front door of Albert P.

Wylie Funeral Home, hoping that I hadn't made a hasty decision. It was late in the afternoon, but I was a few minutes early
for my shift. I rang the doorbell, and as I stood there waiting
for someone to answer, I felt my armpits go damp. I was nervous, but my mother had insisted that I wear a blazer to cover
my shoulders in my sleeveless dress, and the silky lining of the
jacket didn't help to keep me from perspiring in the record-
breaking heat. According to her, it was unprofessional to go to
work with bare arms and legs. She made me wear panty hose
too, but I didn't really mind because I dressed formally all the
time, even at school. I didn't even own a pair of sneakers. But
I sure was overheated.

As I stood there beneath the brown awning bearing the
funeral home's logo, the world seemed dim—even with the sun
beating on my back. For a moment, I felt like a contestant on a
game show, standing uncertainly before door number one. A
perfectly cast shadow stared back at me through the beautifully
etched stained glass. The glow from the iridescent sparkle around
it made me think of Aunt Mary's spirit and provided reassurance
that I wasn't alone. And in fact I wasn't quite alone yet. My
mother was still watching from her car as I waited to make my
grand entrance.

"Can I help you?" a woman's voice called out to me from
a little intercom box.

"I'm here to see Deacon Wylie," I yelled back, competing
with the busy afternoon traffic.

"One moment," she replied. In less than a minute, a tall,
dark woman waved me through the door, where she introduced herself with a handshake. "I'm Angela."

She was wearing a navy A-line skirt and a sleeveless blouse.

A pair of ivory one-size-fits-all stockings covered her legs. I could tell they were from the corner store because the dollar stockings always seemed to sag around the ankles on everyone. I tried not to stare, but this dark brown woman with the Caesar cut didn't seem like she should be working for Mr. Wylie. She was too fashionable, and she didn't have the zombielike, hunched frame of most characters I'd seen on television who worked in funeral homes.

I sashayed my way through the exquisite French doors of the three-story row house. The last time I'd been there I had not looked any further than the room Aunt was in, and now, looking closer, I found that the recently renovated building did not give off the drab feel that I expected. I thought I would see snagged strands hanging from the raggedy carpet and squeaky ceiling fans spinning with layers of dust. I anticipated it would smell like mothballs or have the unmistakable stale scent of old people. Instead, I got a whiff of the familiar aroma of oranges— more like an orange sherbet than a citrusy orange smell. Sweet.

The parlor had clearly been redesigned to attract a modern clientele. Glistening chandeliers dangled from the ceiling in the hallway, and the floor tile seemed too delicate to walk across in my pumps. It was like a very chic hotel lobby, except for the burgundy marquee hanging in the lobby, which screamed mortuary. That felt-covered board required you to spell out the name and service times of the person on view letter by letter. Maybe Deacon Wylie was trying to appeal to the younger crowd, the B-boys who visited the funeral home more than they attended regular church services, by making them feel comfortable inside a mortuary too. But it was also a nice environment for middle-class families who dished out thousands of dollars for a service.

According to the marquee, a funeral was scheduled for the following day, which both intrigued me and made me uncomfortable. I knew I would probably see the dead body of a stranger at some point during my shift. I wasn't afraid to see a fully dressed and made-up corpse in a casket, but what if it was naked and stitched, gushing with all types of icky fluids? That was a sight I didn't think I ever wanted to see. But the time to be scared had passed. My mother had already pulled off, and she was not returning to pick me up until eight P.M.

I followed Ms. Angela, who was strutting up the stairs like she owned the place. The butterflies in my stomach performed a gymnastic routine, and I wasn't sure that my unreliable knees would carry me up the full flight. I grabbed the banister of the winding stairs and held on for life as a whirlwind of thoughts circled in my mind. Who was this woman, anyway? Was she taking me to a room of dead bodies? I sure hoped Mr. Wylie would greet me at the top of the staircase.

"I'm glad you're here so I don't have to keep running up and down these stairs," Angela said to me like we'd known each other forever. I forced out one of my cheesy ear-to-ear grins. My fright aside, I was also thinking that I certainly wasn't prepared to run up and down the stairs in my high heels either. A place this fancy should have a buzzer to remotely unlock the door.

When I reached the top of the stairs, Deacon Wylie wasn't there to greet me, but I was relieved to find I wasn't standing in a morgue either. In fact, I was standing in Ms. Angela's office. She was the office manager and in charge of accounts payable, and later I learned the unofficial staff psychologist. In what seemed to be her usual routine, the thirtysomething mother of three took a seat behind her huge puke-green desk.

The top of that desk was well battered, as though it held a part of every soul that had ever rested in the place. On the left-hand side was a pullout board that listed the phone number to every hospital, cemetery, and black funeral home in our vicinity. These were numbers that we needed immediate access to, numbers that I would eventually memorize over the years. It looked like the contents of a recycling bin had been poured onto the beat-up desktop. Folders and loose papers had bombarded it, and there was one . . . no, two . . . actually, three ashtrays masked as paperweights among the clutter. Sensing my judging eyes, she defended her desk, saying, "Look, people who keep neat desks don't do any work. We work around here."

Then she directed me to take a seat at the desk across from her. The owner of that desk must have been a lazy slouch, because there wasn't one thing out of place. All the papers had been clipped and stacked into manageable piles. Funeral programs were neatly stacked in chronological order.

I picked them up and looked at the names and faces on the covers. A few programs had a picture of praying hands instead of a photo, so I assumed that those people's families hadn't been able to find pictures to include. Suddenly, I saw Aunt Mary's familiar face in the midst of all the strangers. I wanted to ask Ms. Angela what role she had played in my aunt's funeral, but I decided not to bring it up since I hadn't seen her during Aunt Mary's services. We had dealt directly with Mr. Wylie, and I didn't know if she knew he'd worked with my family recently or if she had any idea I was a member of Deacon Wylie's church. I wasn't sure if it was my place to tell her. Overwhelmed by the programs, I put them away and spun around in the chair.

Behind me stood a kitchen equipped with a working gas stove and a fully stocked refrigerator for the two Wylie men, who lived on the floor above. In front of me was a small corridor that served as an arrangement room, where families gathered to make the funeral plans. A big round table and four cushiony chairs were crammed into the intimate space, leaving little room to move around. Flimsy accordion doors provided some privacy, but naturally it was easy for the staff to eavesdrop. When the doors were pulled closed, Mr. Wylie asked his employees to speak in a whisper.

Before Mr. Wylie could afford to lease the whole building, he had leased only the basement and the first floor and made a makeshift office in a corner outside the embalming room. There was no heat, so in the winter he would tuck his hands beneath his bottom to keep them warm. The office was not in any condition for visitors to see, so he took his fancy catalogues and books and went to the homes of his clients to make funeral arrangements. But he'd come a long way since those days, and now the building was his in its entirety.

Ms. Angela grabbed her lighter, lit her cigarette, and puffed away. Then she pulled her chair around and began pecking at the typewriter. She was obviously waiting for me to say something.

"I'm Sheri," I told her. "Did Deacon Wylie tell you that I was coming?"

"He told me that he had found somebody for the evenings."

"Oh, okay. Well, is he here?"

She rolled her eyes and gave me a "Do you see him?" look. "They aren't back from the service yet."

"How long have you been working here?" I asked.

"Since April." She took another puff.

I didn't have to ask much before she began to spill her life story. She began to explain to me how she had been a member of "The Fellowship." I assumed that the Fellowship was a church organization or fraternity of some sort. But she told me that someone she met there referred her to Mr. Wylie because the two of them shared a similar past.

I guess my sitting there reminded her of her first day, because she recalled the morning of her interview with him. She told me that after getting to the office promptly and waiting in the sooty conference room, she thought, *This is some ghetto shit.* Mr. Wylie hadn't arrived yet and had sent in his secretary at the time, who was also his cousin, to size up Ms. Angela. This was something he did whenever he considered a new hire— he'd want to know what she looked like: how she kept her hair, what she was wearing. He didn't hire fat girls because they could not walk up and down the stairs and that was a major part of the job. According to Ms. Angela, she had been dressed to kill in a sharp pantsuit and a pair of blue-and-white two-toned tie-up pumps.

Twenty minutes after the scheduled interview time, the man himself walked in.

"You got any children?" he had asked her. He didn't like to hire women with young children because the hours at work were demanding.

"I have three children . . . but I am about to get married," Ms. Angela had replied.

"Thank you, Jesus." They both laughed. He was relieved that at least she wasn't a single mom.

The two of them talked for what seemed like hours before he asked her when she could start.

"In two weeks," she told him.

He didn't hesitate. "How about tomorrow?"

The next morning Ms. Angela was at the funeral home answering calls.

The doorbell rang and broke her out of her memories.

"Hi, can I help you?" she asked the person on the other end of the intercom.

A man at the door replied that he was there to see the woman on view.

"One moment," she replied.

She slipped on her pumps, extinguished her cigarette in the ashtray, and motioned for me to follow her. My shift had officially begun.

We were back down those stairs in a flash, opening the door. I didn't know whether to wear a smile or a serious expression when I greeted my first visitor, so I decided that I would follow Ms. Angela's lead. But I couldn't imitate the look on her face. It wasn't a smile but an experienced, somber face that said, "Welcome in your time of sorrow" perfectly.

As the man stepped inside, I searched his face for emotion, but it was blank.

"I'm here to see Ms. Ross." He was a tall middle-aged man, still wearing his post office uniform.

Ms. Angela handed him a burgundy pen with the Wylie logo and asked him to sign the register book.

"She was my neighbor." He spoke to us like he knew we

had been wondering, and then stopped to autograph the soft-back register book. I would later learn that if the woman's family had spent a little more money they could have gotten a hardback version of the guest book.

I noticed that Ms. Angela was standing with her hands behind her back, so I dropped my hands from my waist and placed them in the same position as hers. We looked on as he wrote out his name and address. I began to grow impatient since I was eager to see the person behind the door and find out the story behind how she had died.

When he was finished, Ms. Angela opened the two wooden doors and led him into the viewing room. He removed his cap, took a deep breath, and walked toward the casket, which was perfectly centered in the front of the room. When he got close to the casket, he dropped his head in an awkward position. Maybe he was praying or attempting to control his tears; I couldn't tell. He laid his hands on the woman's perfectly propped hands, patting them a few times. I realized I had been standing in that same position less than three weeks ago, smoothing Aunt Mary's chilly hands, but the room looked different now. It didn't seem as big as it had before. And then I heard it, the soundtrack that made my already broken heart crack into tinier pieces. The horns on that instrumental were a killer. I just wanted to reach up into the ceiling or wherever the sound was coming from and make it stop.

I waited for the postman to move so that I could have a better view of Ms. Ross. From what I could see, she looked a little bit older than my mother, so I figured she was somewhere in her forties. Everyone I had known who had died had been well into their sixties or older, and it was unsettling to see the body of someone so young. The woman's skin was still smooth and her lips were pink from lipstick. I didn't see one gray hair in the tightly curled do on her head. But she looked at peace inside her bronze casket. She held a lovely bouquet of yellow flowers that matched her dress, and a nameplate of the same color was sitting in the open head of the casket. She didn't have a fancy plaque like the one Mr. Wylie had made for Aunt Mary. I wondered if he added that touch for special families only.

"How'd she die?" I whispered to Ms. Angela.

"I think cancer. I have to check her death certificate when we get upstairs," she said.

I felt bad intruding on this man's private moment, but I was too curious to look away. And then it happened: the scene, the music—it all caught up with me and I started to cry for this poor dead woman.

The doorbell rang and broke the spell. As more visitors arrived for the viewing, I sniffled a bit and then wiped my eyes, trying to collect myself. Ms. Angela let me answer the door this time, and I tried to attempt the more serious look I'd seen her wear. I welcomed four ladies in and showed them the register book. When they were done signing their names, I waved them into the viewing room with a little hand twirl I'd seen the ushers at church use to signal parishioners to come forward. Once they were in, I stepped back and gave them their space. At first I counted five people in the room, but soon that number doubled. It wasn't long before I completely lost count and the voices in the viewing room began to grow much louder. For the next twenty minutes, people were in and out, but none of the visitors stayed very long, and before we knew it we were back upstairs in the office. *That was simple,* I thought.

Before I could sit down, I heard the sound of keys rattling in the doorway. And then I heard his big voice: "Hellooo." Mr. Wylie announced himself when he walked into the building. His feet quickly shuffled up the stairs, and his son, Brandon, trotted up behind him. Both were wearing black suits. Mr. Wylie walked in first, but my eyes were stuck on Brandon, who looked like a lighter, younger version of his father. I'd had a crush on Brandon since elementary school. He was a few years older, and I was definitely not on his radar back then, or at least I didn't think I was. But a few years earlier, when Deacon Wylie had handled the funeral arrangements for my grandmother's brother, whom I had never met, Brandon handed me a rose as I was standing by the grave site, watching the workers lower the casket. I smiled and said, "Thanks." And he grinned back at me and said, "You're welcome." It felt like the most meaningful conversation that I had ever had with a boy, and I would often think about it when I saw him in church. I kept that rose until every petal dried up, turned black, and fell off. I even used the stem as a bookmark in my diary. It never occurred to me at the time that he was working that day and that when he handed me that rose he was giving it to me to place on the casket before it was lowered into the ground. That rose, as far as I was concerned, was a romantic gesture. You couldn't have told me otherwise.

"Booker! What's up?" Deacon Wylie asked. "You like my place?" He spun around with his arms out. Then he stretched out his hand to give me five.

I slapped his hand and smiled.

"Mr. Wylie, where do you want me to put this?" Brandon

asked about an envelope he was holding. *Who calls their dad "mister"?* I thought.

"On my desk," he answered.

"Mr. Wylie?" Now Ms. Angela was calling him. It was then I realized that all his employees referred to him as Mr. Wylie, which would be a challenge for me since I had spent the last six years calling him Deacon Wylie. He shuffled through the mail, discarding the bills onto Ms. Angela's cluttered desk.

"We got any checks?" he asked. She handed him the insurance payments that had come in. "That's what I'm talking about," he said and smiled.

Then the front door creaked open again and I heard footsteps travel up the stairs. When I looked up, a beautiful young woman with a bob cut was standing in front of me, wearing a black suit that looked like it had been custom-made for her. I remembered her face from the church fan, but she was much prettier in person. Clearly, I was sitting at her desk, but she didn't indicate that I should move.

"No, stay there," she said as she reached around me to grab a bottle of lotion from her drawer. "I'm Chanel Bacoate," she continued. Her name even sounded fancy. Her pumps were at least four inches high. I admired every detail of her appearance down to her neatly manicured nails, and I wondered what this elegant, sophisticated woman was doing working in funeral service.

"The food is here," Ms. Angela announced to everyone. It seemed a bit unusual to take a lunch break in the middle of the funeral home, but the staff all went into the kitchen, where only four chairs were placed around the table. Lunch breaks were hard to come by, so they took them whenever they could, which often meant after leaving the cemetery following the final burial. Though I wasn't hungry, I also didn't want to be left alone. I didn't know my place, so I stood in the doorway and listened to them talk.

Then the phone rang. All eyes looked to me to answer it.

"Booker, get that," Mr. Wylie yelled.

I walked to the other room and picked up the receiver.

"Hello?" I said.

"Albert P. Wylie Funeral Home," Mr. Wylie hollered from the kitchen.

"Albert P. Wylie Funeral Home," I repeated to the caller.

The voice on the other end of the line wanted to speak to Al.

"Please hold," I said, thinking I was doing a good job so far.

I peeked into the kitchen to let Mr. Wylie know the phone was for him.

"Did you put it on hold?" Mr. Wylie called, as if he knew that I hadn't already done so.

I had never used a phone with an actual hold button. I thought covering the receiver with my hand and holding it behind my back was the same thing.

"Tell them I'll call them back."

It was clear that I had a lot to learn. I hoped Chanel was going to be the one designated to teach me.

I picked the receiver back up. "Hi. Mr. Wylie's unavailable. May I take a message?" I said to the caller.

"Tell him it's Ms. Ray-Ray," the woman on the other end of the phone told me. I would learn that Ms. Ray-Ray called often. She referred many death calls to him from around the neighborhood, and they had developed a relationship. I wrote her name down on the message pad; then I ripped the carbon copy off and handed it to Mr. Wylie.

"Put it on my desk," he said as he picked at his chicken.

Answering the phones would be a crucial part of my job. Since grieving people were in search of comfort when they called the funeral home, it was important that my voice sounded compassionate and understanding each time I answered the phone. The tone of the person answering a death call could often seal the deal.

Back in the kitchen, Ms. Angela and Chanel sat at the table like they were dining at a five-star restaurant. The two of them had taken down plates and a set of silverware to eat the fried chicken wings and fries that came in the chicken box. Chanel was eating the ketchup-drenched fries with a fork and Ms. Angela was using her knife and fork to slice the meat off the bone. Brandon and Mr. Wylie had no such formality. They rolled up their sleeves and dug in with their hands, devouring the chicken like they had never eaten before.

As the crew recapped the day, another woman let herself in. Her stern face seemed familiar, and she appeared to be in her early thirties. Then it hit me that I had seen her tiptoe into the sanctuary at church and sit in the pew behind my family. I had never learned her name because she didn't seem like the friendly type and I was always too afraid to turn to her in church when the pastor told us to greet our neighbors. I don't think I had ever seen her smile. She was mostly always scowling at her son for misbehaving in church.

"Booker, this is Marlo. She will be here with you, training

you in the evenings," Mr. Wylie explained to me. I imagined that she would be a drill sergeant and wished again that Chanel were the one training me.

By day, Marlo was a bank teller, but at night she babysat dead bodies and two grown men who required a woman's hand. Mr. Wylie had learned how to turn his personal needs into business affairs. Marlo did the grocery shopping for the funeral home, while Ms. Angela did errands like taking his mother to the podiatrist. Chanel always dropped his suits off at the cleaners.

Marlo smiled when she realized we knew each other from church and picked up the clipboard from Ms. Angela's desk to peruse it for new cases. When she was done she handed it to me.

"Do you know what this is?" she asked.

"A clipboard?" I shrugged with a smile. She obviously thought I was an idiot.

She rolled her eyes and began to explain. "This clipboard has all of the information you need. When someone calls with a question, your answer is most likely on this board."

The sacred clipboard contained forms with information listed in a grid: the case number; name of the deceased; date of death; funeral time, date, and location; and date of the viewing. Most viewings were scheduled for the day before the service, but sometimes under special circumstances a viewing was held for more than one day. The family viewing was usually held before the actual service, while the public viewing was scheduled from four to eight P.M., the exact time of my shift.

"If it's a viewing, you will need to dress up. No pants. Mr. Wylie hates pants," she explained. "When the phone rings, you should say 'Albert P. Wylie Funeral Home' before you say anything else."

"I learned that earlier." I laughed.

She told me that the evening staff member had to wash the dishes at the end of the night. I hoped she was joking because I had never washed a dish in my life.

When everyone was finished eating, they came back into Ms. Angela's office. I waited for Brandon to finally speak to me, but he didn't. We went to the same high school, but he didn't pay me a lick of attention. I was a nerdy freshman with bifocals in the honors course, and he was one of the cool kids at school, with a fancy chain necklace that said "B. Wylie." That's what everyone called him, but to me he was just Deacon Wylie's son.

"Y'all can go." Mr. Wylie informed Chanel and Brandon that they were finished for the day.

"Angela, you can go too. Booker, you got the phones." The fact that he called me Booker made me feel professional, since both of my parents were called by their last name at work.

Around six o'clock Marlo walked me downstairs and we greeted the people who were coming in and out of the viewing. This was the time of day that viewings received the most traffic. One by one they piled in, trampling the peach carpet with work boots, pointy heels, and dress shoes. Some were sniffling, others smiling; some held cards, others came empty-handed. The woman *on the floor*, the term used when a body had been embalmed, dressed, and brought upstairs into the chapel for viewing, had definitely been loved, and her viewing wasn't sad like I imagined it would be. Most of the people in the room shared laughs and fond memories of her. In fact, I may have been the only person who cried that day, and I hadn't even known her.

At about a quarter to eight, Marlo went into the kitchen and ran the water to wash the dishes. Plates covered with chicken bones and hardened ketchup still sat on the table. I helped her clean it off, surprised that adults would leave such a mess.

"Did you get the official tour?" Marlo asked after we finished with the dishes.

"No," I answered, curious about what I had yet to explore.

She promised to give me one the following day. After she turned out the lights in the other room, she flipped through the clipboard and reminded me that there wasn't a viewing the next day and so I did not have to wear a dress.

．．．．

WHEN I arrived the next afternoon for my shift, Mr. Wylie sat on the side of the copper-toned brick building, shrouded in a cloud of smoke. His dingy blue embalming pants and raggedy flannel shirt reeked of embalming potions. It was hard to believe that this was the same man who had no doubt been perfectly dressed in a three-piece designer suit for his service earlier that day. His legs were stretched out right in front of him as if he were sitting in a recliner, and in his right hand he held one of his Tareyton cigarettes. When you embalm bodies for a living, a smoke break is the least you can do to calm your nerves. And Al, who started his mornings at about five A.M.

and ended his evenings of embalming way after midnight, deserved the pack he smoked each day.

In his other hand he held his always buzzing Nextel cell phone, an accessory that he couldn't live without. Even before everyone had a cell phone, he had a car phone in his black Cadillac de Ville. When he needed a casket right away or had to schedule a burial, he just pressed the button and called his staff while he cruised around town. For him, communication was a priority. Not being available to answer meant that he could lose a case, and losing a case meant that he wouldn't get paid. That's why he constantly upgraded his phone, just like his car; whenever a new model hit the market, he traded his old one in.

He kept his little black Rolodex on silent when he was on a service because he knew that his staff could call at any moment to check in with him. He wouldn't dare upset the atmosphere of a "decent Christian burial." Still, most decisions were made only with his approval, so if you didn't get in touch with him, you waited. When Nextel created the walkie-talkie cell phone, he bought one for each of his staff members so that they could communicate with him between funeral services and move like Secret Service men while escorting families to burials.

In Baltimore, black funeral homes take turns monopolizing the industry. For more than a decade, March Funeral Home was the premier black funeral business, with facilities in both East and West Baltimore and a popular black cemetery in Randallstown. But in recent years, the names of overnight sensations began to travel from lip to lip in the black community, and Mr. Wylie's business was steadily growing, making him a strong competitor. Whenever one of Wylie's neighbors stopped at the stop sign on the corner, they would honk their horn, nod their head, or throw up a peace sign to salute the petite gray-haired man. Just by sitting on the stoop outside the funeral home, he became a living billboard for his business.

"Ayyyyyyyyyyy," Mr. Wylie would yell back each and every time, throwing his hands up in a "What's up?" gesture. As he sat on the small ledge with those small legs stretched out in front of him, he listened to the processional of honking horns that drove by. That was his theme music, one of the things that motivated him to keep going. He knew his hood loved him, and he loved them back.

There are some men who get only one chance at life, and then there are those who live and learn and live once again. Malcolm X did it—reinvented himself after years of incarceration—becoming a great leader to African Americans across the nation. In his own small way, Albert Philip Wylie wielded the qualities of a great leader, providing inspiration to the men and women in West Baltimore who thought happy endings could never happen to them. He narrowly escaped the peril that so many of his friends and neighbors continued to suffer and was able to become a living example to many who wanted a better life.

Anyone who lived in the neighborhood had probably attended one of his funerals. If they didn't know about his past—the flashy cars, stylish wardrobe, and hot women—they would never suspect it now. His approachable demeanor made it easy for people to befriend him. He greeted all the young hustlers who stood at the corner store when he walked up to buy his cigarettes. When the fiends came to the door begging for change to feed their families, he would let them wash his fleet of cars or do a few chores to earn the money. When elderly women walked by with their heavy groceries, he greeted them and offered to help. When poor families came to his door crying because they didn't have any insurance to bury their loved one, he gave them a break. He was still a hustler, only this time it was legal.

Mr. Wylie stomped out his smoke and walked over to the car to greet my mother. "Here, Booker," he said, handing me the key to the front door. I was a few minutes early, but he made it clear that my shift had started.

I soon learned there would always be a task awaiting me when I arrived. That day, one of my first assignments was to simply transfer information from the green three-in-one information card onto the all-important clipboard. The green card was a trifold stock card that we used to collect the personal history of the deceased: basic biographical information that was essential to the death certificate, the names of immediate family members, and so on. In case we needed to write a death notice for the newspaper, we needed to have the names of all the remaining loved ones on file. The green card always stayed in the deceased's file folder, and the clipboard had the most accurate information about the client's service.

After reaching into my purse for a pen, I began transferring information from the green card to the clipboard, copying the text in my best handwriting.

When Mr. Wylie came inside and to the office, he picked up the clipboard to check on the next day's services.

"Noooooooo," he yelled.

Ms. Angela and I looked at each other in confusion.

"Where is it?" he asked.

"Where is what?" we asked simultaneously.

"The blue ink pen."

"Oh, I put it in the cup," I responded.

He grabbed the cup and turned it over and then scrambled through the pile of pens, scribbling with each on a sheet of paper to find the one I'd used. Each time he grabbed one I hoped he'd found the culprit, because he looked angrier and angrier. There were at least thirty pens scattered on the desk. My face flushed with embarrassment. I looked over at Ms. Angela, and she just shook her head. Then he found it, holding it up between his thumb and index finger as if it were the tail of a rat.

"Do not bring blue pens into my funeral home. We do not use blue ink pens in my funeral home. We only use black ink in my funeral home."

I learned that black ink was required for the official death certificate, and Mr. Wylie feared that one of his staff members might one day mistakenly write on the death certificate with blue ink, which would make it invalid. Once a doctor had signed the death certificate, there was no room for the funeral home to make careless errors. Doctors were always difficult to track down, and errors on the death certificate could even put a funeral or cremation on hold. The burial transit permit is the last carbon sheet attached to the death certificate and is required by a cemetery for burial. Once we completed our part and the doctor's signature was in place, a death certificate had to be certified by the Department of Health and Mental Hygiene for the official seal. Then it could be used to verify death, open estates, and redeem insurance policies. There just wasn't time for errors when it came to the death certificate.

"Girl, you should have seen your face." Ms. Angela laughed as Mr. Wylie left the room. "I bet you won't do that again."

I was just glad that Brandon hadn't been there to see that episode. I might have cried with shame.

Not long after the pen incident, I was met with another sharp reprimand. Mr. Wylie had asked me to mail off a death certificate for him. I'd decided to use just pens with the Wylie logo on them to be safe, but the first thing I always did was test the pen anyway to be sure the ink was black. I looked on the clipboard and carefully copied the address onto the envelope. Mr. Wylie walked over to the desk and looked over my shoulder.

"Noooooooooooooo. Don't you know how to address an envelope?" He shoved a new envelope at me because I hadn't perfectly centered the name. With Mr. Wylie there were no in-betweens. Your work was either perfect or unacceptable. If you couldn't meet his standards—and many couldn't—he told you that funeral service wasn't for you and then he escorted you off the premises.

After the second time I was met with his fierce discipline, I vowed to be perfect at every task I was asked to complete. I wasn't used to being reprimanded in this way, and I definitely didn't like it. There was a huge difference between my father fussing because I didn't clean my room and Mr. Wylie fussing because he thought I couldn't address an envelope. My father knew I was capable of cleaning my room; I was still proving myself to Mr. Wylie.

· · · ·

THE first time I walked by the chapel and saw the organ there, I knew I would have to return to the chapel alone to check out the instrument and explore the music. I noticed the red Baptist hymnal on top of it and couldn't wait to sing my favorite song. I had seen the chapel one afternoon when I directed a visitor to the bathroom and then again on Marlo's tour. Now, at the end of my first week, I had my chance. The soles of my feet sank into the spongy, peach-colored carpet as I snuck into the room inside the hollow building. I felt the stillness in the air. Marlo was running late and Mr. Wylie wouldn't return for at least an hour, so I had the full run of the place. I was dying to sneak into the private part of the house and Brandon's room, but for now I quietly slipped inside the chapel.

The lighting inside was faint, but natural sunlight crept through the curtains as I took a seat at the organ. The hymnal we used in church was sitting on top of it. Flipping through the pages, I found my favorite spiritual, "Lift Him Up," and started to really bang the keys. I was humming and playing, and I had a strange sensation that someone was watching me even though I knew I was the only one in the building.

As I got to the last verse, I took my hands off the organ and started clapping and tapping my foot like I was the musical director at a Baptist convention. When the song ended, I covered the organ keys and got up to deliver a mock eulogy, just like I used to do when I was growing up. I always loved "playing church" and imagining myself as an inspiring minister. But as I turned to where the podium would be, I had a surprise in store. A dead woman in a metal casket was sharing the room with me.

I jumped away from the bench, barely landing on my feet. I mustered up my courage to look again to make sure my eyes weren't deceiving me, but there she was: A brown woman with dark hair was stretched out peacefully in a rose-colored casket. I was far enough away that I couldn't see the details of her face. It was like seeing a ghost.

I rushed out of the chapel, stumbling over my own feet, and dashed up the stairs. My heart beat ferociously against my chest as I spent the next five minutes trying to regulate my breathing. The clipboard had shown that there was a viewing scheduled for the next day, but no one had told me that there was a body *on the floor.* The image of the woman lying there played on repeat in my mind. I hadn't been alone with a body before then, and I hadn't shown any respect for the dead by playing the organ and putting on a silly show.

A few moments later, when Marlo arrived, she found me sitting at my desk studying the clipboard.

"What's wrong, sweetie?" she asked, sensing my unease.

I shared my embarrassing run-in with her, taking care to leave out the part about my singing performance. I didn't want her to think I wasn't taking my job seriously.

"Are you scared of dead bodies?" She laughed.

"No," I lied.

"Come on." She motioned for me to follow her.

I wanted to show Marlo that I was tough, since she looked

like the type of woman who would clock a mugger before he even had the chance to grab her purse. She led me down the long hallway back to the chapel and then guided me inside to the casket. The woman was wrapped in a shroud, and pearl beads hugged her neckline. She lay with her face pointing up toward the ceiling, and her eyes were sealed shut. Her makeup was flawless and her arms rested across her waist as her hands held a bouquet of flowers.

Marlo walked up to the woman and placed her right hand on the woman's hand.

"See?" she said while caressing the inert hand. I watched carefully to make sure that the woman didn't move.

"Touch her," she said firmly.

I looked up at Marlo's stern face and then turned to the woman in the casket. I wanted to whisper an apology in her ear, but instead I extended my hand toward her. I hesitated at first.

"Go on, feel her face." Marlo urged me to get it over with.

I gently stroked her cool cheek, and the dead woman's pear-shaped face smiled blankly back at me. I would later learn that death smiles are man-made, a minor technique of skin adjustment. I expected to feel tightening in the pit of my belly like when I touched Aunt Mary for the first time, but instead, an inexplicable feeling of peace washed over me. I didn't feel connected to this woman because I didn't know her story.

That wasn't so bad, I thought. Maybe it was Marlo's presence, but somehow I felt safe.

It was a good thing I got my first experience with a dead stranger's body out of the way early on, as most of my afternoons would be spent babysitting the bodies that were on view.

The first viewing (or "family hour") was the hour in which the immediate family members came to inspect the body. In many cases, it was the first time the family had seen their loved one after releasing the remains to us.

I quickly learned that the viewing was like receiving a report card. Families would scrutinize the body and make sure it was in perfect condition. They might request more lipstick. Sometimes they hated the hair or the outfit, which they had chosen themselves. Whatever the reason, if they weren't happy, Mr. Wylie would go back and make changes before the body went on view for the public. He had a distinct style—he made sure not to cake on makeup the way some undertakers did, trying to hide damage or make someone look more dead. But some people couldn't handle their loved ones looking too much like they'd looked when they were alive; it was as though they needed the body to look fake after death for the whole thing to actually feel real. Mr. Wylie would do his best to give them what they wanted to see.

Family viewings were meant to be a private time, but uninvited guests often snuck into the room by posing as loved ones. I understood how someone could break the rules because they couldn't wait to see a friend or lover. The first viewing was also when the balance of the funeral bill was due. If a family was very late, you could almost assume that it had something to do with finances.

When there was a viewing, I was assigned to the front door for several hours at a time. I would open the door and begin with a chorus of "Good evening. First opening on the right." As I stood there, I would absorb all the sob stories. Sometimes if a death was a homicide, I might overhear the backstory or the name of the prime suspect. I would hear wives and mistresses bicker through the open door. Sometimes someone would kiss or hug or even lie on the body, and then I would have to go into the viewing room and make sure that they didn't damage the casket or disturb the corpse.

One day I arrived in my black dress clothes to work a viewing when I heard hushed voices coming from the viewing room. "Don't worry about it—we gonna get them niggas," I heard a husky voice say between sobs. "It's just a matter of time," another voice said.

I couldn't believe what I was hearing. How disrespectful to talk that way in front of a corpse, not to mention stupid to do it in public. I walked quickly up the stairs.

"What's going on downstairs?" I asked Ms. Angela.

"What do you mean? The family's in there for the first viewing."

"Oh! They sound angry. Sounds like they're talking about retaliation."

"Probably," she said, unalarmed, but I was scared. It was pretty clear that the person on view was a homicide victim. Would we be burying the people those two family members were talking about next week?

Just then, the doorbell rang and I went down to let in a girl who was there to attend the viewing. Since I was anxious to see the faces that matched the voices I'd heard, I escorted her through the hall and into the viewing room myself.

I walked in and saw two men standing in front of the casket and a group of women sitting to the side of the room talking softly. The room didn't have the air of sadness that I usually felt around the families. Everyone was too calm. The girl walked up and hugged the men in front of the casket, and when they stepped to the side I saw the dead man, who looked to be in his early twenties. He was wearing a button-down Versace shirt the same shade as his light blue casket. I could tell that his family had spent a lot of money on his funeral, and I assumed that it was drug money. I was sad that he'd lost his life in such a terrible way, but what was worse was that his two brothers felt it was up to them to avenge his death.

CHAPTER
THREE

IN those early days, I couldn't help but leave work questioning God. While death certificates changed hands like loose change, all I could think was that not only had the omnipotent one pulled the plug on the woman who had practically raised me, but he was also snatching the breath of other Baltimoreans without just cause. In a mere four weeks, I had ushered more than fifteen families into the room where loss became real. The more I contemplated it, the more unfair death felt. People—old and young, pruned and baby faced—were withering away beneath the earth's crust. Even after an expensive embalming procedure, they would still decompose into unrecognizable pieces of bone, their families left to worship dirt and idolize marble headstones, their legacy condensed into a few short paragraphs. I wasn't naïve enough to think that people lived forever, but in those moments I wasn't mature enough not to resent God's plan.

It wasn't blasphemy; we were God-fearing people. My sister and I were raised to respect our heavenly father. When we were growing up we were forbidden to use the Lord's name in vain. I figured that if I were ever able to ask Him why so many people were dying, His answer would be similar to my mother's response to many of my questions: "Because I said so."

My grandmother, whom we would sometimes visit in the summers, was also a devout Christian who did her part to put the fear of God in us. If there was a thunderstorm while we were staying with her, my grandma would make us turn off the television and lights, unplug the phones, and sit in complete silence. According to her, thunder was the sound of the Lord speaking to us. With each thunderous roar, we listened to what our heavenly father had to say, and my grandmother sat in her recliner with her arms folded across her chest and her eyes shut like she was praying. I'd just sit there staring at her—too afraid to move or breathe too hard. It didn't matter if we had to pee, cough, or sneeze: We'd better not move a muscle during God's sermon. She made us believe that if we misbehaved during that time, lightning would strike us. I just tried to concentrate because God's language was foreign to me and I needed to translate what he was saying. But now I was having trouble just taking what God was delivering.

. . . .

LATE one Friday afternoon, highway traffic stood still and streetlights patiently waited to flash on outside Wylie Funeral Home. Inside, the staff sat around the kitchen table as usual, sharing a chicken box like a big happy family. The kitchen table was special—it was the heart of Wylie Funeral Home—and you weren't a part of the family unless you'd been invited to dine there. Our proud papa sat in his designated seat. Still dressed in his black suit from earlier that day, he slid off his jacket, hung it on the back of the office chair, and rolled up his sleeves until his embroidered initials disappeared beneath his cuffs. Then he reached into the white rectangular box and grabbed the first piece of chicken delicately, dangling the wing between his thumb and index finger as if he didn't want to mess up his manicured nails. His caseload was heavy, so he was scheduling his personal nail technician, Mr. Bunny, to come in and groom his hands and feet only every two weeks.

Sitting to his right was his proud baby boy. Brandon was undeniably Mr. Wylie's son. Though he was a few shades lighter than his father, his peanut-shaped head was identical. The two of them wore glasses, and when dressed in their suits, they looked like twins separated by a generation. Brandon had not yet mastered his father's swagger, but Mr. Wylie wasn't finished grooming him.

The two Wylie men were already chomping on chicken when I arrived at the table with my plate. I tried to avoid sitting near Brandon. It wasn't that I didn't want to be close to him; I just didn't want anyone else to know that I did—and I definitely didn't want him catching on to my girlish crush.

My indecisiveness forced Ms. Angela to make the choice for me. "Girl, are you gonna sit down or not? I'm trying to eat." Ms. Angela did not pull her punches. I slid into the open seat she motioned to beside Brandon and tried my best to act cool and ignore him.

I was more interested in Chanel anyway. I liked to think of her as an older version of me. We had the same gold complexion and the same style of glasses, and we both wore our hair in a straight bob. She'd even graduated from my high school. But what I liked most was Chanel's ambition. At the age of twenty-two, she was second in command at the funeral home. While she was only Mr. Wylie's apprentice, he treated her like a full-fledged funeral director. She had already graduated from Gupton-Jones College of Funeral Service in Atlanta, Georgia. The Community College of Baltimore County's Catonsville campus was the only school in Maryland that offered a funeral service program. She had even passed the National Board exam, which was a requirement in order to become a licensed mortician. All she needed was one thousand hours toward her apprenticeship and she could take the official exam of the Maryland State Board of Morticians and Funeral Directors and become a licensed director in our state. Without a license, the furthest you could go in the field was a secretary or driver position, which meant anything from driving the hearse to making removals and running errands. You couldn't legally embalm bodies or be solely responsible for funeral arrangements.

Mr. Wylie spent most evenings with a bottle of embalming fluid while vibing to gospel classics. He always waited until the skies were dim and the business of the day had been settled before he slipped into something more comfortable and headed down below, where there was always someone waiting to receive his undivided attention. On nights like this, he'd call Chanel back into work to assist him. The hands-on experience she got during her grueling twelve- to fifteen-hour shifts was incomparable, since many directors were too busy to actually teach their apprentices, and their patience wore particularly thin when it came to women. Most male funeral directors thought the only place for a woman was in the office, so directors hired them to answer phones and run errands. They rarely let them anywhere near the basement, except to style hair and apply makeup. The only women who had real power in the industry were directors' daughters, wives, other blood relatives, or in-laws. If a woman happened to own a funeral home, you could bet that she'd inherited it from her daddy's estate or a divorce settlement. It was tough to climb the ranks to mortuary ownership as a woman if the business hadn't been passed down by a man.

From the looks of it, Chanel could break through the ceiling, and watching her, I started getting interested in the business. She had wiggled her way into a profession that didn't usually accept women, especially those who were young and attractive.

Mr. Wylie knew if he promoted Chanel, he would be seen as a trendsetter, and he knew that having a hot young woman leading his funerals would make him the talk of the town and probably earn him more business. So he vowed to teach Chanel everything he knew. He was training her to rule the world—his world.

There was another reason that Mr. Wylie wanted to take Chanel under his wing. Brandon would be leaving Baltimore to go away to mortuary school at the end of the summer, and with the volume of death calls increasing, Mr. Wylie needed someone he could depend on. He could always see the future of his business, whether it was with or without you in it.

When I heard the sound of the telephone ringing while we

were all eating, I jumped up like it was my snooze alarm and I was late for school. I had already learned that as soon as I walked through the front door, my shift began. It didn't matter if I was early or if Ms. Angela was still on the clock—I was expected to answer the phone. So I didn't bother to wash my greasy hands or wipe my mouth before racing to answer the call.

On the other end of the receiver, a distraught woman whose marital status had just shifted from "loving wife" to "bereaved widow" tried to mask her grief, but there was no disguising the shiver in her voice or the echo of disbelief that bounced through the line. She couldn't fool me; by that time I knew those sounds all too well. It was like a song that you hate when you first hear it, but after a few radio plays you find yourself knowing all the words and singing along. Though it was often a remixed version, the death call was a familiar tune that played in my mind on repeat. Little did I know I was answering the call that would turn out to be the most challenging case in Wylie history.

"Hello, is this Wylie's?" Her voice was urgent.

"Yes, ma'am." I answered in a high pitch, hoping that the innocence in my voice would help give her a bit of comfort. Mr. Wylie and Brandon always answered death calls with a sweet southern drawl.

She cleared her throat and with a much stronger voice said, "I need you to come pick him up."

I followed with another "Yes, ma'am."

"My husband, he died in the house."

She sounded like a resilient woman and reminded me of my mother, who was too put together for her own good. Maybe she'd known her beloved husband was gravely ill and she'd already made her peace. Or maybe she was in denial or had too much pride. Whatever helped her resolve, she was keeping her tears tamed for the duration of our call at least, and that was more than I could say for most of the other widows I had talked to.

"Have the police been there yet?" I asked while grabbing a pen.

In moments like these, I felt like a 911 operator. The call was *that* important. The information was *that* classified. The subject was *that* sensitive. I had no time to test pens or search beneath the clutter for a message pad. The world stood still when the voice of grief was on the other end of the phone. You forced yourself to memorize names and numbers if you had to. But most important, you reached deep down inside to muster up every bit of compassion you could.

Answering the phone was an art, a technique that I quickly mastered. This wasn't so for many of the women Mr. Wylie hired. They easily found themselves standing in the unemployment line because they couldn't perfect the death call. Their voices weren't welcoming enough to secure the sale. They weren't swift enough to grab the receiver in between the first and second ring, which was a Wylie rule, so that impatient family members wouldn't be tempted to call another funeral business.

If you couldn't master the greeting, then you certainly couldn't get through the rest of the call. The most important part was allowing the person on the other end to tell his or her story. *They killed him! He had been sick for a long time. We don't have any money. My grandmother said if she died, call Wylie first.* You needed to train your ear to listen through the hollow cries of folks whose lives had just been shattered. Every now and then, you needed to shift your disposition so that you could understand the short-fused, bitter callers who could test your patience.

Sometimes you'd get comparison shoppers who only wanted prices. They'd ask, *What's your cheapest funeral? Do you have a payment plan? We don't have any insurance; can you help us? Does that include cemetery? What about a limo?* The questions went on and on. No matter what, it was our responsibility to keep them on the line until they could speak to Mr. Wylie, or we had to figure out a way to seal the deal on our own. So we baited them like hostage negotiators and said whatever it took to keep them talking to us a little while longer. We'd walk them carefully through our price lists and services and try to sniff out what would be most appealing to them. It was important to be knowledgeable and make them feel we had only their best interests at heart.

I learned quickly that nothing turned Mr. Wylie off more than someone calling for prices. It wasn't so much the price checking; it was when someone called him because they thought a competitor was too expensive. He never altered his fees to secure a case, no matter how bad he wanted it. That didn't mean he wouldn't help lessen a family's financial burden once they signed with him. But unfortunately, we did not offer a payment plan, and Mr. Wylie expected a family to have paid in full by the time of the first viewing. I thought his policy sounded harsh at first, expecting people to come up with thousands of dollars on such short notice. Death is often unexpected, and most people are saving money so that their kids can go to college, not so they can bury them. However, Mr. Wylie had a business to run, and if he relied on IOUs, he would be dead broke.

Uninsured families suffered the most, but insurance isn't foolproof. Some people got screwed because they owned accidental policies and in the end they died naturally after paying years of premiums. But the biggest problem is that the average person is unaware of the contestable clause that is scribbled between the fine lines of a life insurance policy. If the policy is less than two years old, the insurance company has the right to contest, and in most cases, they do. They summon medical records and coroner's reports. They want death certificates, police reports, and newspaper articles. This all tends to hold up the process, which meant that Mr. Wylie would not get paid for a while or sometimes wouldn't get paid at all. After he lost his payment a few times, he stopped accepting contestable policies altogether. Some other directors were willing to take the risk, but we weren't.

When families planned their arrangements with us, things could quickly shift from *The Price Is Right* to *Let's Make a Deal*: If you choose this package, you will receive a new car . . . I mean casket. This was especially so in the case of the social service voucher. If the deceased was receiving a monthly check from the Department of Social Services, then he or she was allowed six hundred and fifty dollars toward the funeral service, but the funeral could not cost more than fifteen hundred dollars. A fifteen-hundred-dollar service was equivalent to our least expensive burial service, and so a family would be left with a balance of eight hundred and fifty dollars. The body would be embalmed, dressed, and casketed, and a small chapel service would be provided. For all other customers, our least expensive service was about three thousand dollars at the time. Both services included a K-Flair casket, a bluish gray felt-covered casket that Mr. Wylie called a "blue dinghy." It felt like it was made of cardboard. I hated that the blue dinghy was the only option for some of the families we served.

The rock-bottom deal we offered was cremation, which was only eleven hundred dollars. At the time, cremation was an act of desperation for a black family, the last resort. You could assume that they didn't have enough money to pay for a funeral. But many families were too proud to cremate their loved ones, even if they were broke. So they borrowed money, asked for donations, and even sold chicken dinners to raise the funds for a decent service.

After quickly scribbling all the pertinent information from the widow on the phone, I handed the receiver to Mr. Wylie, who would give her a price quote and his usual assurance that we would handle the arrangements with care.

"We're praying for you," he said sincerely before hanging up the phone. He lit his cigarette and kicked up his feet on Ms. Angela's desk. "Load up," he called out to Brandon, signaling him to prepare the station wagon for a removal. The woman's husband had been cleared by the police already, probably because of a preexisting condition, I imagined.

As soon as the call ended, it was time to get to work. The death call was the moment that we lived for. Seconds later, we would spring into action to prepare for the removal. Just like every other task at the funeral home, prepping the car was a methodical procedure. It involved a thorough inspection of the van and a wipe-down of the stretcher before it was loaded into the car. It all took about five minutes, which was just enough time for Mr. Wylie to give us any interesting details about the case, finish his cigarette, and give directives for the hours ahead. "They ain't got no money. He's a veteran. Died in the house . . ." These were things that we needed to know so that we could start the process.

According to Mr. Wylie, an unpleasant scene had awaited him and Brandon at their destination that particular night. A mob of frantic family and friends flocked the front porch like vultures, praying and pacing and petitioning the heavens. When they noticed the funeral director walking toward the door, they dispersed to the side, creating a path for the Wylies.

The tiny row house on Appleton Street was a hoarder's heaven. Mr. Wylie greeted the woman he had spoken with on the phone, then headed into an infestation of filth and clutter that made the air fetid and difficult to breathe. Dust from the staircase clung to his pant legs as the deceased's daughter led him up the stairs. Inside the bedroom there was a rank odor, which more than likely came from the containers of waste that lined the bedroom wall. Bloated and stiff, a six-hundred-pound man sank deeper into the crevice where he had shut his heavy lids the night before. He had been dead for hours, and the lack of ventilation certainly didn't help matters.

But the smell wasn't the problem. The real issue was how two slender men who together totaled just over a third of this man's dead weight could lift him. While there were several men from the family gathered outside, it would have been un-professional to ask six of them to come inside and serve as gurney bearers. "You only get one chance at funeral service," as Mr. Wylie always said, so the Wylie men set out to prove their strength.

I'm sure Brandon did not want to spend his Friday evening panting and sweating. House removals were usually an in-and-out process. But when you're the boss's son, you're always on call.

Back at home base, I received a call from Mr. Wylie.

"Pull out the green book and see what funeral directors are available to help me," he said, clearly nervous about the situation.

The green book was like our ghetto Rolodex. Mr. Wylie was responsible for the organization of the book, but Ms. Angela was in the process of revamping it. The three-ring binder contained the telephone numbers for every one of Mr. Wylie's contacts, both business and personal. It wasn't in alphabetical order like a normal phone book or even organized by category like the yellow pages; rather, it had a system of its own, hewed from Mr. Wylie's labyrinth of a mind. For instance, if I needed to find Kendall Shoats, the electrician, his contact information would not be under S for Shoats, K for Kendall, or E for electrician; it would be under H for home improvements.

After compiling a list of potential helpers from the scattered book, I started to make calls. Because it was after six, most of the other funeral directors didn't feel like lending a hand, or in this case all of their upper-body strength. Working in the business is tiring and time-consuming, and making a removal on a Friday night certainly didn't sound appealing, especially since Saturday is one of the busiest days for funerals. Even the men who drove for us and would normally help out at the drop of a dime for a small paycheck weren't willing to pitch in that day. Finally, after I called funeral home after funeral home, I found a few volunteers.

Once the other four men arrived, they had an even playing field, or at least an equal amount of weight. They all tried to lift the body together and determined that they could do it. But the dead man had been confined to his bedroom for years, and even with a team on hand, moving him still presented a problem: How would they get him from the bed to the gurney and then through the narrow doorway, down the stairs, and out of the house?

According to Mr. Wylie, the group spent the next twenty minutes deliberating. They considered dragging him down the stairs, but out of respect for the family, they agreed that calling the fire department was the next best option. The firefighters arrived with a crane, attached the man to a stretcher, and slowly hoisted him out the window. After they lowered him to the ground safely, they helped get him into our van.

Removing the body was only the first major challenge of this case. When we got him into the embalming room, we discovered that the embalming and dressing tables could not support his weight. Mr. Wylie made a makeshift embalming table by putting a broken door in the basement atop two extendable casket stands. To embalm him, we needed to use twice the amount of fluid that was normally used. A man his size could not fit into a traditional casket, and his grave site also had to be dug double wide. So the family had to pay an extra fee for an oversize casket, and the cemetery charged them double for two plots. Our facility could not even accommodate his service—the combined weight of his body and the casket were much too heavy for our casket lift, so we had to hold his viewing at the church up the street. The process was going to be costly and complicated.

The dead man's wife was distraught, and she called a couple of days after the removal to tell Mr. Wylie that she was struggling to write the obituary to insert in his funeral program. Mr. Wylie told her not to worry; he would send one of his staff members over to help. As I listened, I thought for sure he'd send Ms. Angela on Monday, so I was shocked when he grabbed his keys and motioned for me to follow along. I grabbed the sample obituary guide that we handed out to every family and followed right behind him, even though I wasn't dressed to represent the funeral home in public. It was a Saturday and we didn't have any viewings scheduled, so I was wearing a pair of jeans and a blouse.

I arrived at the house to find a heavy woman sitting outside on the porch. I could see the deep pain in her eyes. It was a look I'd already come to know well.

"This is Sheri Booker. She will help you write the obituary and anything else you need," Mr. Wylie explained.

"Thank you, Mr. Wylie." She hugged him in relief, and then she turned to me. "And thank you, baby." She grabbed me in her arms.

"I need to get back to the funeral home. Call me when you're done," Mr. Wylie said, pulling his keys from his pocket.

I cut my eyes at him. I didn't know he'd be leaving me there alone. But he just smiled and walked away.

"He sure is a nice man," the widow said as she watched him head toward his car.

She called inside the house and asked her grandson to bring me a chair. It was humid outside that afternoon, but it felt much hotter inside the house.

There's a lot of pressure in writing someone's legacy, some-how condensing their life story into an eight–and-a-half-by-eleven-inch folded booklet, a souvenir journal for friends. I was so sick of reading the same old boring obituary over and over again:

> On March 12, 1989, (insert name) *left this world after a lengthy illness*. (Insert name) *completed his education in the Baltimore City Public School system. He gave his life to Christ at an early age. In* (insert year), *he married* (insert spouse) *and from this union they had* (insert number) *children.*
>
> *He leaves to mourn . . .*

Everyone used that basic template. I wanted to write something different, so that when this man's grandsons and -daughters pulled out the program five years later they would have a living artifact and a sense of their ancestry. I wanted the obituary to really capture who he was. But there's not much to write about a man who spent many of his years locked away eating himself to death, more familiar with Oprah and Jerry Springer than with his own children or grandchildren. But I still felt he deserved to have his story written. If nothing else, I figured naïvely, I could write about his love for food.

"He wasn't always that big, you know," the widow ex-plained before I even asked her any questions. "When you're around someone so much, you don't notice the pounds adding on. Then one day you look up and they weigh a ton." She looked embarrassed.

She called into the house again and asked her grandson to bring out a picture. In the photo was her younger, much thinner husband, posed in front of the house, exactly where we were sitting.

"We can use this for the program," I told her, and began asking her questions about her husband. As she talked, I picked up little tidbits, such as his love for the Baltimore Orioles, that were usable for the obituary. She said he'd always wanted to go to a game, but even though they were the local team, it was too far for him to travel.

"Where's Pop-Pop?" A little boy who looked to be about three years old poked his head out the door.

"He's gone to heaven now."

"Heaven?" he asked in amazement. "They got baseball up there?"

"They sure do. Go on back in the house so I can finish talking to this lady."

Writing that obituary felt like a promotion to me. Since the print runs were only two hundred copies, funeral programs were fought over and some people made bootleg copies. They hung on bulletin boards of apartment buildings and workplaces. They became a part of a family's archives, and sometimes they were mailed all over the world. I was now a scribe of these important documents, who made house calls.

· · · ·

THAT evening I wondered if a stranger would have to write my obituary when the time came. Would the closest person to me in the world be unable to describe me on paper? Would my family be so overwhelmed with grief that they would be at a loss for words? What would be my legacy, my end-of-life story? That night I decided to record my own history.

I had stopped writing in my diary the day my mother read it around the time of Aunt Mary's death. But that wasn't even the first time she'd read it without my permission. When I was ten, she found a journal I was writing, and in it I had called my sister every curse word that I knew at the time. My mother's punishment was to make me look up each word in the dictionary. I knew not to try to hide another journal from her, but since I no longer had a place to keep all my secrets about the boys and other things in my life, I kept them inside. One day, I decided to be smarter than my mother. I took out a sheet of loose-leaf paper and began writing my feelings in the form of a poem. Then I worried that she might read that too. So I rewrote it, only this time I wrote the poem backward. I wrote the first verse at the bottom of the page on the right-hand side, and the next line above it until it spilled over into the next column. When I was finished, there were three columns, all written backward. It took me some time to adjust to the unique style of writing I'd made up. Sometimes when I read the poems back to myself, I would be totally confused.

But that night when I wrote my first obituary, I wasn't writing to outwit my mother; I was writing to find my own peace.

Sheri Janine Booker was born in Baltimore, Maryland, on the ides of March 1982 to William and Mary Booker. She departed this life suddenly on . . .

She received her education in Baltimore City Public Schools, where she was an honor roll student.

She sang with the Peabody Children's Chorus, the North Avenue Choir, and N Full Effect. She also took ballet, tap, and jazz at Dance Dynamics for seven years. She loved reading, poetry, and playing computer games.

She gave her life to Christ at an early age and was a member of Greater New Hope Baptist Church, where she sang in the youth choir and was leader of the youth ministry.

At the age of thirteen, she became employed at Youth R.I.S.E. and traveled the state speaking to students about service learning hours. She was employed at Wylie Funeral Home.

She leaves to mourn her loving parents Mary and William; one sister, Chantá, two grandmothers; her grandfather; her boss, Al Wylie; her dog, Lucky; and a host of aunts and uncles, relatives and friends.

I realized how blessed I was and how much I had done in my fifteen years, especially since I'd read obituaries while working for Mr. Wylie that weren't longer than two paragraphs. It was like saying they were born . . . next paragraph, they died.

After sitting down with that man's wife, I realized that a person's true legacy is measured by the impact that they leave on the world around them, not the words of grieving loved ones. Sometimes good deeds go unwritten but their traces are left in the hearts of others.

About a month later, while I was reaching in the kitchen closet to get a bottle of ketchup, I knocked my mother's cookbook onto the ground and a few sheets of yellow legal paper fell out of it. When I picked them up and read them, I recognized my mother's handwriting. I realized that she had written a draft of her own obituary, and my heart dropped. I wanted to ask her why she'd done something like that and why she kept it hidden in a cookbook in the kitchen closet, but I couldn't.

. . . .

SOON Mr. Wylie began to realize I had talents other than writing that I could bring to my work to help him. One Saturday morning, he called me into his office. There was a funeral in the chapel that morning and the family needed a soloist, so he needed me to step in right away.

"What do you want me to sing?" I asked nervously. I needed time to prepare.

"One of those hymns you sing in church every Sunday."

Um . . . , I thought. " 'Amazing Grace'?"

"Yeah. That's fine."

I went into the bathroom and softly practiced to myself. Then I went downstairs and grabbed a program from one of the drivers to see where I was scheduled to sing.

Downstairs, Mr. Wylie was starting the service and I saw with relief that there were fewer than thirty people seated in the chapel. I had performed in front of crowds much larger than this and even sung at Aunt Mary's funeral, so I thought this would be a piece of cake.

When I sang in church, I would close my eyes to feel the power of the song at its most dramatic moments. But as I stood there before a weeping crowd, I realized that today I couldn't get lost in the music. I was used to people standing up, waving their hands, and encouraging me to sing in church, but this time I wouldn't feel the audience sweeping me away. There was only heaviness. This time I wasn't just performing; I was paying tribute to someone's life.

Not long after that, Mr. Wylie called me into his office again. I pulled up a chair in front of him.

"What did I do now?" I asked while trying to replay every task I'd worked on for him recently in my mind. I was afraid to make a mistake that would upset him. I even repeated his directions to confirm them: "So you want me to look in the folder and get the green card and call Ms. Johnson for her social security number?"

"Yes," he would say.

"What if she doesn't answer?"

"Leave a message or keep calling until you get her," he would say, looking at me as if he wanted to say "Duh!," but he was always patient.

"I don't want you ringing my doorbell no more," he said another time with a serious face.

I was puzzled. Sometimes it was difficult to tell if he was joking or if he meant what he was saying.

"You need a key," he said with a grin as he opened his drawer and handed me a key to the front door.

I had been working there for only five weeks. Not only did he trust me to represent him with clients and take major roles in the services, but he was also giving me the key to his world, his place of business and residence. That was major, and

I was honored, especially since I hadn't even gotten a key to my own house until earlier that year. I rushed to the supply closet and grabbed one of the key chains with the Wylie logo. I vowed then to be the best funeral home girl in the world. For the next nine years, I wouldn't let that key out of my sight, under any circumstance.

• • • •

THOUGH I knew a lot about Mr. Wylie from seeing him in church on Sundays and seeing him at work in the evenings, I learned pieces of his personal life through discussions with Ms. Angela and the other women who worked at the funeral home. That's how I found out that Brandon was an important factor in his dad's divorce. The second Mrs. Wylie hated when Brandon and his friends hung out at the house because they were loud, messy boys. Mr. Wylie, on the other hand, encouraged the boys to hang out there because he wouldn't have to worry about them getting into trouble in the streets.

Ms. Angela wasn't shy about talking to anyone about anything, really. Most afternoons you could find her with her ear glued to the phone. If you heard a "yeah, girl" or a "listen, let me tell you," you knew she was probably dishing out advice to one of her girlfriends. But it could have been one of our vendors or clients just as easily. Even the woman at the Chinese carryout around the corner loved her. She became friends with everyone and often kept in touch with families long after their business was finished. She probably missed her calling as a therapist. You knew she loved you even when she cursed you out, and I had definitely been subjected to Ms. Angela's good ole curse-outs on more than one occasion. She'd really chew me out if I was late, but I soon learned to arrive promptly at four to spell her and start my shift, even though she never left on time herself. But what I admired most about Ms. Angela was that she lived by a philosophy of always "keeping it real." She was brutally honest about everything. If she didn't like your outfit she told you, "Oh no! That ain't going to work." If your hair looked a mess, she'd say, "Girl, what you doing coming in here with a nappy head?"

Ms. Angela wasn't shy about parading around details of her own life either. In typical Ms. Angela fashion, she often described the very explicit details of her sexual escapades with her husband to Chanel. I always happened to be sitting there when the discussion came up, and sometimes I wished my mother was there to send me to my room, because I really didn't want to hear those conversations. I know I should have felt privileged to be let in on the girl talk, but I was fifteen. I was learning to handle death but not interested in sex talk from people twice my age.

· · · ·

THE walls at Wylie's were paper-thin, and voices traveled as swiftly and smoothly as the spirits that embodied the parlor. A whisper sounded like a yell. We knew when a family was broke and when a family had gone overboard on spending. We heard families in anguish, and just as often, we listened to them bicker.

One afternoon, I arrived just in time to overhear a family making the arrangements for a young homicide victim. His three sisters were there with the mother of his child. If his girlfriend had been married to him, she would have been able to make the arrangements herself, since a surviving spouse has the primary right to possession of the body and the burial rights. But in this case, his sisters were paying, so even though his girlfriend had strong opinions, they insisted on making all the decisions.

Mr. Wylie was finally able to mediate the group's discussion and bring them to an agreement, but after the arrangements were final, they went outside cussing and fussing and a fight almost broke out. In the end, the sisters agreed to let the girlfriend compose and pay for the programs only because she felt so strongly about how it should be done.

The next day she brought me the layout. Instead of just dropping it off, she demanded that I sit down with her and allow her to explain it, so I brought her upstairs to the arrangement room. On the front of the program she wanted three photos: one of him in the middle, one of herself on the left, and one of them together on the right. In the inside of the program she wanted more photos of herself and some with her and her children. I thought, *Sweetie, you will be on the cover of your own funeral program sooner than you think.* I felt uncomfortable about the layout, but Mr. Wylie gave the green light for it to be printed since this had been the agreement. The deceased's sisters were not happy with the program on the day of his service, but in the end

it was a small thing, and the rest of the service went off without
a hitch.

· · · ·

IT was a joy to laugh in the funeral business, when ninety
percent of your day was spent straight-faced and serious. Joking
with families rarely went over well, so we had to entertain one
another. Very rarely was it at the expense of the deceased's family,
but there was one case that summer that took us all by surprise.

When I got to work that day, Ms. Angela insisted that I go
straight to the viewing room. On display there was a woman
who had nubs for arms and legs. She had little fingers attached
only to her right arm, and little toes on both nubby feet. A
munchkin-size woman, she was in a cute little dress and a
braided wig. Her face was made up really pretty, but the sight
of her left me shivering. Before I could get a word out, Ms.
Angela spoke. She looked at me, bursting: "You believe this
woman has six kids?!

"I'd like to know who fucked her!" she shrieked and burst
into laughter.

Ms. Angela could make a joke out of anything. And
though I didn't want to laugh, because six children were now
orphaned, the whole scene was so absurd.

Mr. Wylie's cousin, Cindy, who also worked with us,
came in to chat. "Hey, I know her. That's the lady from the
supermarket who picks up the meat with her feet! That's why
I stopped shopping there!"

By then, Ms. Angela and I were in stitches. When they finally left the room, I walked close to the casket and asked that woman for forgiveness. I did not want to be haunted for the rest of my life.

● ● ● ●

I'D grown attached to Chanel, but soon she was leaving us. Famous for putting her makeup on using the hearse's rear- and side-view mirrors, one afternoon she accidentally sideswiped someone with the hearse while perfecting her face. It seemed clear that she was slipping. She and Mr. Wylie had a heartfelt conversation, and in the end she realized she could not balance the long hours and nighttime embalming for the rest of her life. Besides, she had promised herself that she would have a Mercedes-Benz and a mink coat by the age of twenty-five, and at the rate she was going at Wylie's, that was not going to happen.

Even though Chanel deserted him, Mr. Wylie would make her the measuring stick for future apprentices, and losing her left us all devastated. Hers was the first name to go in what became known as "the urn of employees past" during my tenure there. I'm not sure where it came from, but one day when I arrived at work there was a porcelain jar on the kitchen table with the words "Ashes of Problem Employees" engraved on it. Whenever Mr. Wylie fired someone, Ms. Angela would write his or her name on a little sheet of paper and place it in the "urn." It was our little joke.

The end of summer was near and I could not fathom the thought of returning my key, something I had earned. I had a proposal for my mother and Mr. Wylie. Since Mr. Wylie hadn't found a replacement, I offered to continue working on the weekends.

"But you got school," he said.

"I know, but it's the weekend. Just Friday and Saturday."

He took one of his long pauses. "Ask your mama."

I promised my mother that a part-time job wouldn't interfere with my schoolwork, and she agreed to let me stay on. In that one summer, I'd seen more death than most people see in their entire lifetime, but I knew I wasn't finished with it yet.

CHAPTER
FOUR

WORKING in a funeral home was like working for the CIA or FBI. All the things that make you human get tucked away in your desk until after your shift is over. And when it comes to the funeral business, becoming that shell means you stop crying. Not crying makes you a hero.

It took me some time to stop becoming emotional at viewings. During my first six months, I couldn't enter the viewing room without shedding copious tears for people I didn't even know. I wept for old Mother Jackson whose fluid-inflated body was squeezed into a small blue-cloth casket because her family couldn't afford a bigger one. I sobbed and snotted all day for the fourteen-year-old girl who hanged herself because she couldn't get along with her mother.

The tears seemed contagious. It was the moment when I saw someone else lose it that got me every time. I saw people bawl so hard that their glasses fogged while tears fell down their face, landing in the creases of their neck. People would mumble, "Lord, please," and "Why? Why? Why?" between their hiccupy swallows. The noises of sorrow would echo across the room, strong enough to make your entire upper body vibrate.

Even as a very young child, I could not stand to see someone suffer. My sister tormented me growing up, but whenever she got in trouble, I felt sorry for her. When a mischievous boy tripped me in the sixth grade and caused me to seriously hurt my knee, I wouldn't tell the principal because I didn't want the boy to get suspended. I never laughed when someone fell; I hated to see someone in pain.

But I will never forget the day I stopped crying. There was a Ms. Norman on view that afternoon. She was a school principal like my mother, and I figured that the foot traffic would be heavy that night as former students and co-workers would line up to pay their last respects. In my mind, educators deserved a special place in heaven, right beside police officers and veterans.

I had gotten to work in just enough time to have a few moments alone with her before her family arrived. I always liked to take a peek at the body I was guarding beforehand. It helped me prepare myself for the hours ahead.

At exactly four P.M., I walked Ms. Norman's family into the chapel and then stepped outside the room to give them just enough privacy. But as I watched from outside the door, I caught the eye of Ms. Norman's husband as he walked away from the casket, his face distraught and streaked with tears. All it took was eye contact with one set of glossy eyes to make me cry. Of course, the chapel music alone was enough to make anyone lose it. The horns crept up on you and snapped your heart open.

I felt a single drop start to roll down my face, when Mr. Wylie walked in the front door. He immediately went into the viewing room to greet the family, and as soon as he extended his hand to the husband, the man broke down. Mr. Wylie stood there strong, but watching them together, I cracked.

Mr. Wylie walked out of the room and heard me sniffling. He grabbed a box of tissues from the register stand and confronted me sternly.

"Look at the wall. Look at the wall. That's what you do when you think you need to cry. Crying is unprofessional. How can you help these families if you are out here crying too?" I knew he was serious, so I reprogrammed myself to smile at the sound of a sniffle and to head for the door the moment I saw tears starting from glassy eyes. Ninety percent of the time this technique worked. In fact, it worked one hundred percent of the time when the deceased was a stranger.

"This is just a business," I told myself over and over until it had been washed into my brain. I convinced myself that death is a blessing, that the person who died is the lucky one. To be stuck here on earth—now, that's suffering.

I wore many hats during the viewing hour. Sometimes I was a girlfriend to the people who needed to tell their stories. I was the accounts payable department to the families that needed to make a final payment on their bill. I was an interior decorator, positioning floral arrangements around the room. I was a church usher, passing out tissues and using stick fans to cool down emotional people. At times, I was even a referee, breaking up fights between angry lovers and friends. I never knew which roles I would play on any given day, so I always wore comfortable shoes, kept my pockets filled with tissues, and wore shoulder pads for those who needed someone to lean on. At the end of the day, I couldn't account for the number of souls that got lost in my bosom.

There was something magical about me to those who were grieving. Maybe it was the fact that I was so young that attracted people to me, but whatever it was, I was beginning to see that I had the power to affect their lives.

. . . .

THE afternoon that I found out that the son of my mother's childhood friend Patricia had died, I knew the strength I had developed would be tested. Patricia had gone to Catholic school with my mother, and she was on the deaconess board of our church. I saw her at church a lot and was very fond of her. She'd always greet me with a hug, ask about school, and tell me what a gorgeous girl I was. She and Mr. Wylie were good friends too.

A few days earlier, Patricia had walked into her son Laurence's bedroom to wake him for school. When he didn't respond to her voice, she shook him while screaming his name loud enough for the neighbors to hear, figuring he was just being like every other teenage boy is before the school day. But it would have taken much more than her frustrated attempts to get him out of bed; what she really needed was a miracle. During the night, an undetected heart murmur had overridden his system, causing it to crash. Her beloved son's bed was now a cooling board. He was seventeen, only two years older than me.

While this year would be the most memorable of my high school experience, Patricia's son wouldn't be so lucky. His face would be absent from the class yearbook. There would be no date to senior prom and no graduation. The year that was supposed to be filled with milestones would be remembered with a headstone.

Over the last months, I had seen the inexplicable pain of loving moms burying sons of all ages. Regardless of who their sons had become, the love these mothers showed for them was unconditional, pure, and sacred. There were some mothers who blamed themselves for not providing a strong father figure or for working so many hours to keep the bills paid. Others felt shame for accepting the drug money and looking away when their sons broke the law. "I should have sent him down south to live with his grandmother," I heard one mother say when she buried her baby boy.

But Patricia knew she'd raised a good boy, and the fact that his future was so bright only sharpened the pain of her loss. Laurence was a handsome boy, tall and slender. He had avoided the streets of Baltimore, which were swallowing young boys by the dozen, and was set to receive an athletic scholarship in the fall.

I hadn't been there during the week, when Mr. Wylie had made the funeral arrangements, but as usual, Ms. Angela gave me a full report. Patricia, quite frankly, was wearing everyone out. There were customers at Wylie who were pretty hands-off about how the services were conducted, who trusted Mr. Wylie enough to let him make all the decisions. Then there were people like Patricia who needed to control every single aspect of the process.

"Girl, this woman from y'all church is getting on my last nerve," Ms. Angela said in frustration. "Every five minutes she's calling with another question. I can't get anything done." She sounded fed up. Patricia had requested to change the casket four times and seemed to have a million other special requests. Mr. Wylie had even gone to her house several times during the week just to discuss her concerns face-to-face. He was sending a limo to pick her up for the viewing the next day, a service that we no longer offered.

That evening, Mr. Wylie spent all the hours of my shift in the basement as he carefully dressed the body. He recognized Patricia's fragile state and didn't want her to have one concern on his end. He took pride in all his work, but he needed this to be perfect.

The next morning I was filled with angst. While I'd grieved for plenty of strangers in the time that I had been there, I couldn't prepare myself for the moment when I would have to work with a family I knew personally. I'd been doing okay so far—at the viewing the night before, mourners had been sobbing in every corner of the viewing room, but I'd kept a mean mug on my face, staring at the whitewashed walls like I was in solitary confinement. Before I left home for the funeral, I gave myself a pep talk. Standing in front of the mirror while brushing my hair, I told myself firmly, "We don't cry! We look to the sky." It was corny, but I needed some words of encouragement and something else to think about to make it through the day.

Both Mr. Wylie and I were on edge as we set up the chapel

for the first viewing. I knew I wasn't allowed to wear my feelings on my sleeve, but that didn't mean they weren't tearing me up inside. Before we knew it, it was time to bring the body upstairs. I waited for Mr. Wylie in the viewing room while he set up the body in the basement. It was hard enough for me to work with Mr. Wylie during setup because he was so picky; everything had to be positioned perfectly. But that day he also gave me the extra-delicate task of operating the casket lift. After he signaled that the lift was ready, I pressed the green button to activate it and the casket magically rose from beneath the floor. It was important that I lift the casket slowly, so that it wouldn't shift and hit the sides of the wall, causing damage, or, worse, slide off the lift. Although the wheels of the table he was on were locked, the casket wasn't strapped in. When the lift stopped, I gave Mr. Wylie the all clear that the casket had made it upstairs undamaged, and he ran up into the viewing room. I grabbed the bottom end of the casket and helped to transfer it from the portable stand to a formal wooden casket stand.

"How does he look?" Mr. Wylie asked after we positioned the body.

I walked closer to the body, thoroughly examining it.

"His lips look a little dry," I replied.

Without a word, he ran downstairs to get his lip kit. He respected my opinion enough to take the note, and we all wanted to do our best work that day. While he was gone, I stared at the boy in disbelief. His porcelain-smooth skin glowed beneath the casket lamp, as if it had been glazed in butterscotch, and there was a slight smile on his face. I did not want to believe it was Laurence lying inside that open casket, but I was holding his nameplate in my hand. I reached inside the casket and placed it on top of the open panel.

"I just saw you in church, like, two weeks ago," I whispered to him. "How did this happen?" I kept trying to remember every detail of the last time I'd seen him. I tried to imagine what had actually happened that night.

Mr. Wylie returned with his lip container and applied a shine to Laurence's lips. He lifted his hand and smoothed the uniform Laurence's body was dressed in and pulled his arms to make sure they would stay in place. Now the body was ready.

The next thing we needed to do was create the atmosphere. The room was already bombarded with so many floral arrangements from classmates, co-workers, teammates, and friends that we'd need an additional vehicle to cart them off the next day. We had no space for the easel where it usually went, at the head of the casket, so we placed it in front of the fireplace. On it was a plaque, the kind we made for our special families, the ones who spent more than five thousand dollars. I'd made it the evening before, framing his photo and carefully centering the gold-plated letters that spelled out his name.

The room was almost right. The only thing missing was Gloria Thompson's sorrowful instrumental *Glory* album. I went in the back hallway and pressed play. As "Blessed Assurance" floated from the speakers, I waited for the family to arrive.

The limo pulled up in front of the building and Patricia stepped out of the car with the grace of a movie star. But this wouldn't be a stroll down the red carpet. It was more like a walk down the plank. The moment I saw her face I wanted to break down, but I stood there and smiled as sincerely as I could.

Patricia's sense of fashion had obviously not been affected by her grief. She draped the bottom of her full-length mink coat over her arm as she walked up the parlor stairs, to make sure it didn't drag on the ground. A mink headpiece covered her head, but strands of her ruby red tresses still managed to flail in the wind.

"My baby! My baby!" she yelled, and my heart sank. I was staring grief dead in the eye, and the stare it gave me back reminded me of just how ugly it was. If my job didn't mean the world to me, I would have walked away right then and there. I wanted to go home and have my own mother console me. Instead, I clenched my fist tight and stood there like a statue.

"Lord, you sent me an angel," she continued to call out. "Look at my angel." I turned around to see that she was staring directly at me.

"My angel," she said, kissing my cheek softly. "God sent you to me. Mm-hmm."

Then she yelled, "Thank you, Jesus! Thank you, Lord!" like she had just felt the Holy Spirit. Her trembling hands clutched mine like a small child at an amusement park, squeezing hard as the sweat on our palms started to mix. Her mother, husband, and daughter were trailing somewhere in the background.

"Now, where's my boy?" she asked.

"Right this way," I answered, pointing toward the viewing.

"Thank you, Jesus. Thank you, Lord." She kept saying the words every few seconds as though she was in a trance.

If she had been crying, it would have been so much easier, because I was now immune to it. But I had never seen this kind of behavior before and it made me uncomfortable. She was thanking God and her son was lying in a casket. I could feel my eyes welling, but I fought to control myself. I clenched my teeth tighter, swallowed hard, and stared at the wall until my eyes became numb. I started to think of places that I could hide my tears—safely stored on a handkerchief in my pocket or deep within my bosom. I would swallow them if I had to. I just couldn't let Mr. Wylie see them should they happen to fall.

"Thank you, Jesus. Thank you, Lord." Her chant got stronger, more rhythmic. I needed her to stop saying those words. What could she possibly be thankful for at this moment?

"Thank you, Jesus. Thank you, Lord," she continued as we walked, still holding on to my hand desperately.

I picked up my pace. I just wanted to get her into the viewing room where Mr. Wylie was waiting so she would release me and I could run to the bathroom and let it all out, all the pain and sorrow it felt like I was carrying for her.

Mr. Wylie stood at the entryway and ushered us into the room. His face was stern, his movements precise. He could see that I had become her crutch, literally holding her up.

"Thank you, Jesus! Thank you, Lord!"

She was crouched down to the ground, but we still had a ways to go before we made it to the front of the viewing room.

"Hallelujah," she yelled. I could feel the emotion running through her as we got closer to the casket.

Her knees trembled every few steps we took, and she squeezed my hand to balance her weight. We were like one be-ing, totally synchronized. I moved where she moved. I breathed when she breathed. If she had fainted, I, too, would have fainted. So when she began to belt out her chant again, I couldn't help but repeat it with her.

"Thank you, Jesus. Thank you, Lord. Thank you, Jesus.

Thank you, Lord," we repeated over and over until we were in front of the casket. The rest of her family followed us.

There he was, stretched out in a full couch casket with his baseball uniform fresh and crisp. A full couch casket only has one lid, which revealed his entire body from head to toe. Shoes were only needed when we had a full casket. Patricia was silent long enough for her daughter to let out a chilling scream that caught us all off guard. The tears poured from her eyes and she picked up her chant again. Her daughter's screams became the background track to her song.

Mr. Wylie walked out of the room, leaving me there to fend for myself. I wanted to call out to him, but I couldn't make my words hit the air, so I just held on tight to Patricia. Now I needed her just as much as she needed me. When she finally freed my hand, I started to back away, hoping I could get safely back upstairs to the office. But she looked back at me with pleading eyes and reached out as if to say, "Don't leave me." I was helpless. For the next hour, Patricia held me hostage.

I resented her for calling me an angel, because angels protect people and provide comfort. Angels use their wings to swoop in and save the day. Angels wipe away tears; they don't fight their own. I had done nothing angelic that day.

• • • •

A few weeks after that funeral, my mother called me in to the dining room to talk. We usually had our heart-to-hearts in the kitchen beside the stove while she did my hair. Every two weeks, I washed my natural hair and used the blow-dryer to comb it out into a huge Afro. Then my mother would part my hair into small sections and apply grease before heating up a heavy metal comb on the front burner of the stove, wiping it with a rag, blowing on it, and pulling it through my coarse strands to press the hair straight. Sometimes the steam would hit my scalp and cause me to jump. All the while, we talked about everything going on in our lives.

But it wasn't time for my hair appointment, and I started to get nervous because the dining room table was usually where all the business took place in our house. We had made Aunt Mary's funeral arrangements sitting at the dining room table. As we sat together, she pulled out an envelope that contained a series of X-rays. They revealed that she had fractures all over her body from where cancer had eaten away at her bone, allowing marrow to seep into her bloodstream.

She told me the doctor had given her only five years to live, and this was the fifth year since her diagnosis. I thought back to the obituary in the kitchen closet. The fact that she was telling me just days before her expiration date made me angry. She hadn't told anyone else except my father, and for the last five years, she had walked around knowing that she could die at any moment. I don't know what made her tell me that day, and I didn't ask. She acted as though it was the kind of conversation we had every day, while I sat there with my eyes glued to the wall.

I was not prepared to face another loss, but again I swallowed my feelings. My mother had been sentenced to death and it was something I had to live with.

Now I knew for sure that it was no coincidence that I ended up at the funeral home. It was supposed to happen that way. The moment I came to terms with death, my fate would be that I would experience it in the worst way. But though I became superstitious, I refused to believe my mother would die that year. God just wasn't cruel enough to take both of my Marys.

In the weeks that followed, I pretended that my mother had not shared her prognosis, and we all went back to work. That's how we dealt with our issues in my family. She looked healthier than other people, though she had become accustomed to hiding what was really going on.

Then one morning, as she was heading down the stairs before school, all of a sudden I could hear her panting deeply. I ran out to see what was going on as she stood there frozen. Later we'd learn that one of the bones in her spine had collapsed. She couldn't speak or call for help. I had no idea what to do. I yelled for my father and he came running and grabbed her from behind. Very carefully, he stretched her out on the floor while trying to secure her spine. I could see that she was in a tremendous amount of pain, but she managed to motion me closer to her as I knelt over her body, and she forced out a few words.

"Go to school. Have a good day."

I hated her for saying that, but I knew it was the only thing I could do. My father took me to school, but I couldn't focus. For a split second in class that day, I imagined her funeral. I knew Mr. Wylie would give her the treatment of a preferred client and I would be there to oversee the process. Now that I was an insider, I could make sure she was prepared perfectly. I wanted her to be buried in a special casket—one like the father of our school's basketball coach, who was also a funeral director, had been buried in. It had a glass top. And I wanted her buried in her nightgown because that's what she wore for my dad. I envisioned a horse-drawn carriage leading the procession—I had seen it done—and a big venue for her service, so that all her former students could pay their respects. As much as I tried to rid my mind of these thoughts, they came unbidden.

What I couldn't imagine was my life without her. My sister and I were never close back then and I wasn't sure that we would ever be. My father was helpless without my mother. We couldn't even eat dinner until she came home from work at night. She was the matriarch of our extended family; even her siblings thought of her as more of a mother than a sister.

As soon as I got home from school that day, the first person I called was Mr. Wylie. He came to the hospital that night while my father and I visited, using his funeral director's card to get him in after official visiting hours. When he walked into my mother's room, he playfully pulled the sheet over her face.

"You won't get this body," she whispered from underneath.

We needed that laugh, but we needed the prayer that he offered that night even more. From then on, I knew I could call on him and he'd always be there.

A week later, my mother was released from the hospital. She went to work the very next day and so did I. I vowed that death would not keep taking the people I loved away from me. I was determined to master it.

CHAPTER
FIVE

BALTIMORE had become a metropolis of death. The blackened streets were often stained with blood, roped with yellow tape, and draped with guilt and shame. Warning shots no longer ricocheted through the air like fireworks. A new breed of marksman was hitting his target. *Gunshot wound to the head. Multiple gunshot wounds.* Whatever it took to make sure the victim never breathed again. Bullets and black-on-black violence caused the pool of men that I should have been dating to shrink each day. Every time I turned around, there I was, ordering a nameplate for another one. I'd know immediately just by looking at their names—Dante, Jerrell, Tavon, Rasheed—that they were young homicide victims. Many of them had criminal pasts; some were just in the wrong place at the wrong time. The majority were under thirty. More and more of them hadn't even earned a high school diploma. They'd be warned by their praying grandmothers and hopeful aunties and often whisked off to church for intervention. They'd give their life to Christ, attend a few services, and memorize the lyrics to Kirk Franklin's crossover gospel hits. But when the streets called, they always answered. I once saw a boy walk down the aisle of a church, vowing tearfully to dedicate himself to God after a convincing sermon by the preacher. Two weeks later, that same boy was in our basement.

Often the shooters were just babies themselves. Whether they'd suffered their own loss of a loved one, succumbed to drug abuse, or had their spirit broken through incarceration, they never grasped the value of life. Some had fathers who were locked away in prison or had been gunned down or mothers who were strung out on drugs or out on the streets doing what they needed to do to get a fix. They were young men who raised themselves because their grandmothers just couldn't do it. And so when they were old enough to become errand boys for the local dope dealers or to be initiated into one of the local gangs, they found something to kill for. The streets were so deadly that people started calling the city "Bodymore" and "Murderland." We weren't living in "Charm City"; it was "Harm City."

Even in cases where a gun was not the weapon, the autopsy results still read "blunt force trauma to the head," "multiple stab wounds," or something else tragic and inhumane. Mr. Wylie was often left to perform major reconstructive work, like a surgeon suturing the bodies that had been hacked open by a medical examiner. Although he wasn't saving lives, he was saving face, literally, restoring their physical features for the afterlife.

Gangbangers and dope dealers were not the only ones

caught in the violence. There were many innocent bystanders too: the flashy boys with real jobs and nice cars who were killed over a botched robbery or carjacking, the young guys whose only sin was having good taste.

Our tidy little corner with the lovely canopy didn't fool anyone; the Wylie funeral parlor fell right in the middle of it all. My father slept with his police radio on, and I could hear the 911 calls from the neighborhood come in through the night. I'd strain to listen to the cross streets when I heard a homicide called in to see if we had a chance of getting the body. The calls were almost always from the neighborhoods surrounding the funeral home, and the perpetrators that my father had to interrogate in the middle of the night had probably walked past our building earlier in the day.

The view from my office window of the surrounding vacant row houses revealed a whole new world to me. A gang of students walked the block terrorizing passersby, and B-boys bopped through the neighborhood rapping to tunes that blared in their earphones, wearing fresh butterscotch Timberlands and Nike Air Force 1s on their feet. Young mothers, some who looked to be about my age, pranced through the neighborhood carrying one child on their hip, one in their belly, and another in a stroller.

And I loved soaking it all in. In my parents' attempt to give us a better life, they'd kept us far away from the action of the streets. I'd hardly stepped from my own front porch to walk alone in our safe neighborhood. My bedroom wall was plastered with *Lion King* posters, and I spent my Friday nights with encyclopedias and note cards. I was the studious, innocent baby of the family my parents expected me to be, but I felt like I had missed out on the very experiences that had made their childhoods rich. The West Baltimore that they grew up in was long gone. They'd both managed to escape (unlike many of the people they had grown up with) before crack took its toll and the affluent families moved out of the neighborhoods. Some of their childhood friends ended up in jail, some ended up on welfare, others ended up on drugs, and some ended up downstairs in the basement of the funeral home.

My father's family still lived on the Westside, and when I visited my grandmother, Big Mama, I had a taste of all the things I longed for. I ran through the alleys of her neighborhood playing Hot Buttered Bean with the rest of my cousins, jumped off porches, and climbed walls. The permanent scar on my chin came from a day of play in the hood. But as I got older we stopped visiting Big Mama's home as often, and I lost that connection. However, I didn't lose my curiosity. I was infatuated with the hood. Many of my friends and family members grew up in environments similar to Gilmor Street. And while they all wished to escape to my house for sleepovers and weekend getaways, I always wanted to run to theirs. I dreamed of buying penny candy and Now and Laters from the corner store, soaking my chicken box in "saltpepperketchup," and letting *yat gaw mein* noodles from the Chinese joint swell in my stomach.

I couldn't disguise that I was from the other side of town. All my friends told me that I didn't sound right when I cursed. People who called the funeral home often thought that I sounded like a white woman. Even Ms. Angela made fun of me and called me a librarian on days when I styled my hair in a bun and wore my gold-rimmed glasses. The other days she called me Sister Bertrille because she said I acted like a nun. But I wasn't holier than thou and I wanted everyone to know that.

Still, I didn't speak the language, and with my lack of rhythm I didn't walk the walk.

I certainly didn't think I was better than the people in the neighborhood, but I knew that I was different. They knew the darkest side of death, and it would leave them scarred for life. They'd easily become bystanders, witnesses, and participants but tried hard not to become snitches and informants. Some were misunderstood. The only reason their pants hung low was because their secrets were that deep. Others suffered from paranoia, afraid that they could be next to die because they'd seen the walking dead: skeletal bodies of loved ones they knew wouldn't make it much longer on the streets. They'd felt real death, not the pretty packaged version that we sold every weekend.

I was an alien in this world, but it was changing me. My mother started saying I was getting a smart mouth. "I see you're talking your Gilmor Street talk," she'd snap when I'd get out of line. My tough talk was even starting to get me in trouble at school—one time my Spanish teacher kept telling me to speak in *"español . . . español."* And I sassed back, telling her that "if I *knew* how to say it in *español,* I would have *said* it in *español.*" Speaking the language of the streets, especially Gilmor Street, gave me new confidence.

Working at the funeral home legitimized me. It earned me cool points and a newfound status at the lunch table; no one could come close to my stories. It never once crossed my mind that spending my weekends at the funeral home was creepy.

While my friends were stocking shelves at Walmart, I was ripping the toe tags from corpses—or at least that's what I told them.

. . . .

SOMETIMES it hit you in the face that we were in the hood, and we weren't exempt from the craziness that went on there. One night, Mr. Wylie and I were holed up in his office. I was still in the jeans and Timberland boots that I had worn to school since we didn't have a viewing scheduled. As he sat at his desk with his face hidden behind a tall pile of bills, I worked across from him designing an advertisement for a souvenir journal.

"Get me an ashtray," he said, sending me off into the other room. His desk was usually covered with them, but that day he had sent them all to the kitchen to be washed. When I returned, the pile of bills had shrunk as he scribbled his autograph on check after check.

The doorbell rang, shaking us out of our quiet rhythm. I figured it had to be someone coming to settle a bill, a walk-in, or someone just dropping by with any kind of request you could imagine. I ran down to open the door, and a stout woman stood before me, hovering an inch or so above my height.

"I need to see the undertaker." She was dressed in baggy jeans and an oversize button-down shirt, the type that neighborhood kids wore. Her round belly flopped over her pants. Short untamed dreadlocks had grown wild on her head like a patch of weeds. She had masculine features and smelled like

93

she'd bathed in a bucket of funk. Each time she opened her mouth, I smelled chitterlings or sour milk or something rotten.

I tried hard not to judge the families that came to us this way. While most of the families we served were working-class, we also had very poor families show up at our door. We didn't discriminate at Wylie Funeral Home. Most of the time we just held our breath until the money was in the bank.

"He's on a call. Can I help you with something?" I baited everyone before actually calling Mr. Wylie down. His time was valuable, and if it was a matter that I could handle, I should just as well handle it. But most people didn't want to talk to me.

"I need to talk to him because this is where I'm going to die," she said, looking over to the chapel as if she knew the specific place where she wanted to be laid out. Still, I just assumed she wanted us to handle the services, and since my shift was almost over and I knew Mr. Wylie would have made me sit down with her to record her green card information, I suggested that she come back the next day. I planned to send her home with some literature to read about preparing her own funeral. She appeared to be in her late twenties or early thirties, way too young to be planning this alone. Most women we buried were at least over forty. I figured she had just found out some bad news from her doctor. Maybe she had a terminal illness. I wished more young people took this initiative to think about their desires if they died.

"Oh, okay!" I smiled brightly, delighted that she had chosen us. "Well, you need to set up prearrangements with us and we can get you started on a payment plan for your service and burial. Let me get you one of our packets. How about you come back tomorrow morning and we can get you all set up?"

"No! I'm going to die here tonight." She caught me before I could run upstairs to get her packet.

"Um . . ." I searched her face for a sign that she was joking, but her eyes only revealed terror, and her lips quivered. I waited for her to retract what she'd just said, hoping she would erase the panic that she'd invoked in me.

"My father and my friend were both in that room, and that's where I'm gonna die," she continued. It was clear she was on a suicide mission, and I was worried that she might not want to die alone. Because her shirt flared out at the bottom, I couldn't tell if there was anything in her pockets. I didn't know if she was armed or had a razor blade or pills. There was a possibility that she was under the influence of something, since it takes a lot of balls to walk into a funeral home ready to die. Each day I walked in there, and I still wasn't prepared to face death, especially not my own.

But here I was, stuck in the small corridor with this crazy woman. She was twice my size, but I could probably outrun her, I thought. There was nowhere for Mr. Wylie or me to escape. I would've had to tackle her to get through the door she was blocking, and the door leading to the basement was at the other end of the hall. I thought about calling Mr. Wylie, but I was too afraid. Deep down I didn't want to leave her alone to hurt herself. The more she talked, the more suicidal she sounded.

"Um, I don't think you can use that room tonight. You should come back tomorrow and we can figure things out." I knew those weren't the right words to say. It sounded like I had offered to assist in her suicide. Standing so close to her, I saw my own life flash before my eyes. She seemed like the type to kill me first and then finish herself off.

Contrary to what people might think, a funeral home is not the ideal place to come to die. The funeral home is a place where the dead come to be reincarnated and where loved ones come to find closure. A motel room would have served her just fine. She could have ordered room service for her last supper, and best of all, she wouldn't have had to pay the bill. The park across the street also would have worked. It was quiet and peaceful. I'm sure she didn't know that a father and son resided here and that the building was a historic landmark in West Baltimore. It didn't need to be tainted by her woes. If she chose to kill herself in our building, she would kill our business.

I hated her in that moment: first, for not having the decency to bathe and groom herself in her last moments on earth, and second, for having the audacity to think she could choose when and where she would end her life, and that place and time was during my shift.

"Well, let me see if the director is off the phone." I tried to gain control. As I turned to walk up the stairs, Mr. Wylie poked his head down.

"You need me?" he asked.

"Yes, Mr. Wylie . . . um . . . this young lady wants to die . . . here . . . tonight." I was trembling, and my big eyes stretched wide.

He began to walk down the stairs and I began to walk upstairs, securing a position behind him. I wasn't sure if I should call the police or not.

"Ma'am?" he asked in his southern drawl.

"That's right. I want to die in here tonight—"

"Not in here, you don't," he cut her off.

"My father and friend was in there, and I'm tired. That's where I'm going to die."

"I don't have time for this foolishness. You need to go."

"But . . ." She reached into her pocket to grab something. I retreated back up the stairs, but it was only a sweat rag to wipe the beads that had burst out on her forehead.

"I'm not playing with you. You have to leave." He put his hand on his hip.

I could not believe that he was saying that to this unstable psychopathic killer who could potentially end our lives. I worried that if he angered her, she would snap and kill us all. They stood there staring at each other in silence. Then she looked at me and then back at him.

"Man, fuck y'all," she yelled as she turned and walked out. He slammed and locked the door.

"Shucks, I don't have time to play games with these people. What she think this is?" Mr. Wylie talked as he marched back up the stairs.

"Mm-hm," I mumbled beneath my breath, still in shock.

She wouldn't be the last mentally unstable person who showed up at our front door. There was one man who always came around begging for bus fare to get his children home. He was cross-eyed and smelled like booze, and never once did I see a child with him. I never gave money to beggars because most evenings I was there alone and I didn't want to risk being robbed if someone thought there was money in the house.

But for the residents of the neighborhood, we were a one-stop shop—the church, social services, the Salvation Army.

People came to us with utility turn-off notices in their hands, boxes of Girl Scout cookies to sell, and raffle tickets for charity. When someone needed a job or wanted to send their kid to college, they rang the doorbell asking for donations. Because funeral directors dress well and drive luxury vehicles, everyone figures they are rich. They are revered as the premier entrepreneurs; their status falls between politician and preacher.

Mr. Wylie didn't take his place in the community lightly, and he believed that everyone deserved to be treated with dignity. I remember a case where I saw just how much heart he had. It was a slow day at the funeral home, and Mr. Wylie came into my office with instructions.

"I need you to go downstairs and get the history information. They don't have any money."

"How much are you going to do it for?" I asked.

"No money! I'm going to do it for whatever they give me."

In the arrangement room, a young grandmother who didn't even look old enough to have kids of her own sat sobbing one of those snotty, nasty cries. Her two-month-old granddaughter had died eight days ago and was about to be moved to the Anatomy Board, a place where unclaimed bodies were taken and used by university students. The bodies that ended up there were sad cases, Jane and John Does, people with unknown relatives who had been evicted from the hospital after occupying a morgue space for too long, or in some cases, like this one, people with families who couldn't gather enough money for a funeral.

The babies' parents sat stunned, clearly only teenagers. The grandmother tearfully answered all my questions, as if she herself were the mother. She told me they had just moved to Baltimore the month before and they were flat broke. I told her not to worry, we would take care of everything, and she just had to do her best to come up with the cash. We treated this case with the same respect and integrity with which we treated all the others, even though we knew there was a strong possibility that we would not get paid. Mr. Wylie ordered the standard white baby cherub casket and covered the rest of the expenses, including the cemetery plot, the obituaries, and the minister. In the end, the parents could come up with only one hundred dollars.

On the day of the funeral service, the family arrived at nine o'clock for a ten o'clock service and sat in the chapel while we set up the chairs. The service lasted only about a half hour. After the service we found out that the family had no transportation to the cemetery and that they had walked several miles to the funeral home. So Mr. Wylie had them squeeze into his Cadillac, and they held the cherub tightly on their laps while he drove them to the cemetery. It was then that I understood the importance of all the work we'd done that week, or that month, for that matter. Providing closure for a death that made little sense to a family with no means was a true gift.

CHAPTER
SIX

NO one doubted my capabilities when it came to handling the responsibilities of working in the business. Whether I was hosting a viewing or using tweezers to perfect the placement of letters on a memorial plaque, I mastered most tasks on the first attempt. But if it had been up to me, the repair shop where Mr. Wylie remade and polished the bodies would have remained off limits to me for my entire tenure. "The basement." Just hearing those words used to put the fear of God in me. "I'll be in the basement," Mr. Wylie would tell me before he disappeared for hours at a time. Draped in old disposable clothes, he often instructed me to hold all his calls and rushed to his cases before rigor mortis could set in.

I didn't know if it was science or magic, but Mr. Wylie was a master at bringing the dead back to life. Somehow bruises, scratches, and even open wounds and bullet holes disappeared in his care. All I knew was that my dad had sternly ordered me to stay out, and the fact that Mr. Wylie had never invited me beyond the threshold confirmed my suspicions. Whatever went on in the basement was not meant for little girls to witness.

But it wouldn't be long before I was faced with the part of the job I dreaded most. On a Saturday morning, I found myself sitting alone in the one room that was usually filled with life, Ms. Angela's office. It had been nine long months since I'd started at Wylie Funeral Home. Mr. Wylie was out on a service, and as he had done dozens of times before, he'd left me there to handle things on my own. I didn't mind because he was always a phone call away, but the silence could be deafening at times. When you are alone inside a funeral home with nothing but your own thoughts keeping you company, your fears loom about with the spirits. Every creak sounds like a voice. There weren't any bodies on the floor for viewing that day, so the chapel was empty, but when I checked the clipboard, I realized that there was a body still on the premises.

The funeral home was a maze of rooms—sixteen to be exact—each with a personality of its own. The viewing room, which also converted into our chapel, was always somber. Whether it was completely empty or filled with visitors, it always had a heavy air about it. The arrangement room, on the other hand, was designed to have a lighter feel since it was where Mr. Wylie turned on his charm and sense of humor to make the families comfortable. But it was Ms. Angela's office that kept all of us sane.

Each floor had three spacious rooms and one bath. Had the funeral business not worked in his favor, Mr. Wylie could have flipped it into a profitable apartment building for three families. I had explored three levels of the building, becoming familiar with the nooks and crannies, the lighting and heating, the phone and intercom systems. I had reached the closest level of comfort you can have when you work inside a funeral home, but still, I hadn't ventured into the basement.

At one point during the morning, I heard a delivery truck come to a stop just beneath my window on the side of the building. I guessed it was Batesville Casket Company, arriving with a casket for us, the first stop on their route. We used the Indiana-based company for most of our high-end funerals. One of their caskets usually tipped a family's bill over the five-thousand-dollar mark. They offered quality wood and metal selections and twenty-four-karat gold-plated caskets and glass tops. They also customized caskets by engraving the outside lids and inside panels. If a family member played golf, for example, you could get an embroidered panel of golf balls and clubs to put inside the casket top. Some models even had keepsake drawers just in case someone wanted to bury their loved one with something special.

On a normal Saturday morning, if Mr. Wylie wasn't there, he called for his morning check-in. Like most supervisors, he wanted to know if I had arrived on time, but more important, he wanted to dictate a list of instructions of all the things he needed me to do. That's why whenever I heard his big voice on the other end of the receiver, I grabbed a pen.

It was after nine thirty and I hadn't heard his voice or seen his face, which was an indication that he was engrossed in an important conversation with a client or lining up a family for a service. But this was the wrong day for him to be busy. I needed to know how we were going to get the casket inside the building without him being there.

I called him while I waited for the delivery guy to ring the doorbell, but it went straight to voice mail. Then I paged him with a 911 page, because in my mind, I had a real emergency on my hands. Caskets were delivered to the entrance that led directly to the basement, and I had promised myself that I would quit before I set foot down there. Every other time a casket driver had made a delivery, Mr. Wylie sent one of the brawny men who worked for him to transport the container inside. With no one on-site, this time was sure to be difficult.

The casket driver stood at the front door waiting for me to answer the intercom. I thought the longer I stalled, the longer I had to devise a plan—one that didn't involve me leaving the safety of my office.

"Hi. Can I help you?"

"Got a casket for you."

"One moment," I answered.

Then I called Mr. Wylie again. No answer.

My imagination was in full force, and I felt ashamed just thinking about the possibility of seeing dead bodies left completely exposed. It was like I would know all their secrets—a glimpse of the stretch marks that they desperately tried to disguise for most of their lives, or the shriveled penises of men who had bragged about their size. It was bad enough that I read their death certificates, but being in the basement would be borderline intrusive, and quite frankly, it wasn't in my job description.

However, there was a deliveryman waiting to bring an expensive casket inside, and I had to make the executive decision about whether to let him in or be fired when Mr. Wylie came back. As frightening as Mr. Wylie's wrath seemed, the basement still scared me more.

Deliveries entered the basement from the side of the building, since the ramp there made it easier for caskets and even gurneys to roll in and out. Except for deliverymen, only the people who worked on bodies were allowed downstairs. That meant Mr. Wylie, his apprentice, his assistant, and sometimes a driver were allowed to help move a casket or unload the van. Chanel was the only woman I had seen go down to the basement. I had never seen Ms. Angela, Marlo, or Mr. Wylie's cousin Cindy go to the basement up to that point.

I left the driver waiting for at least ten minutes before he rang the bell again. I was running out of time. I whispered a little prayer, "Lord, give me the strength," then stormed through the funeral home with a burst of fury to hide my fear. I ran down the first-floor hallway, passed the chapel where I'd already encountered dozens of bodies, and prepared myself to go down under. I swung the door open, reached my hand inside, and switched on the light. Then I pushed myself beyond the doorway and down each step until I felt my feet reach solid ground.

There I was met with the nauseating scent of formaldehyde, which reminded me of the frog and the pig that we had dissected in biology class. I stared straight ahead, avoiding the dimly lit room to my left, where I assumed the bodies were kept, and followed the blueprint in my head to the area where I thought the door would be. The room in front of me was empty except for the casket lift, a few scattered boxes, and an L-shaped tool on the floor. It wasn't fancy at all.

I finally reached the basement door and opened it to find a handsome young man, his chiseled biceps poking out from beneath his uniform, standing there with a look of disgust.

Lifting the heavy metal boxes was doing his body good, and I was distracted for a moment by the thought of him using those strong arms to protect me. I smiled, relieved to have fresh air greet me and grateful to have another soul in my presence.

"Do you have a church truck?" he asked.

A what? I thought. I was introduced to new terminology every day, but "church truck" was completely foreign, and my mind could only imagine an image close to the literal meaning. A church on wheels?

"I don't even know what that is," I said, completely embarrassed.

"There has to be one in here," he said. He was so used to Mr. Wylie or one of the assistants meeting him at the door with the contraption that he didn't know where to find it on his own. Our eyes searched the four corners of the room. Whatever a church truck was, it wasn't immediately evident, and I refused to search beyond that corridor. Then I spotted a closet door.

"Do you think it's in here?" I asked, as if he were the funeral home employee. I hoped that the church truck and only the church truck was tucked inside. I motioned the guy to walk with me as I tiptoed toward the closet. He reached beyond me, grabbed the knob, and opened the door. Inside was the four-wheeled roller he had been looking for.

He pushed the church truck out the door and quickly returned to his vehicle, which was full of caskets he needed to deliver. It was clear he thought I had wasted enough of his time. After hopping inside the vehicle to get the plastic-covered casket that belonged to Wylie's, he measured the space to make sure the casket wouldn't hit the sides of the truck and get damaged. He had delivered for Mr. Wylie long enough to know Mr. Wylie would send it back to the warehouse for any little scratch. Before he pulled out the joystick that lowered the casket to the ground, he unfolded the church truck until it was the same length as the casket itself.

"I need you to grab that side," he said, expecting my tiny self to help him lift that heavy box. I was in a pair of platform heels, not the typical shoe for lifting caskets.

I positioned myself in front of the casket until we were directly in front of each other. Our eyes locked. Then on his signal, we lifted and placed the casket onto the wheeled stand. While his end was perfectly positioned, my end was unbalanced. I had hoped that one of the men walking up the street would volunteer to assist us, but it was too late and my side was already tilting over. As I struggled to align it properly, the deliveryman ran to my side to help evenly distribute it.

Once he helped me get the casket inside, I lifted the plastic and checked for scratches. There were none, just some dust. I signed the release and he was off.

As soon as the door shut, I ran up two flights of stairs into my office. I'd made it out of the basement, my innocence still intact.

Over time, I learned that casket deliverers weren't the only men who would need access to the basement during my shift. Joe, the exterminator, came by to spray for pests every few months. And like me, Joe was petrified to set foot in the basement. Yet he didn't mind going into the vacant buildings next door to spray for rodents.

While I still wasn't the most comfortable being in the basement, I always had to take Joe by the hand and lead him in, standing nearby while he sprayed. One afternoon, after ushering him down into the subbasement, which you had to enter through the basement, I had to leave Joe while I answered the front door. When he realized that he was alone, he ran up the stairs about as fast as a graying old man could but not before falling and skinning his knee on his way back to the first floor.

．　．　．　．

AS the months passed, my savings account began to swell. Each Friday when I got paid, my mother took my check and deposited it at the bank. She wanted to teach me to be a good steward of my finances. With her permission I was allowed to withdraw money every now and then, but I didn't spend much money on clothes because all of my attire was still the same color: black. After Akcita Rich told me that I couldn't match my outfits a few months earlier, all black seemed safe. That was until another girl at school told me that my blacks didn't match. According to her there were different shades of black—shiny rayon black, gray black, fresh cotton black, ashy black, and brown black.

I was well into my sophomore year of high school, and the weekend shift had not interfered with my grades at all. In fact, I was still on the honor roll and had been recruited to be a part of the International Baccalaureate program, a new college-prep curriculum that had classes more advanced than Advanced Placement. All the nerds had applied for it. If you passed all the exams at the end of your senior year, you could enter college as a sophomore.

I could never quite plan for a Friday night at the funeral home. If it was a quiet night, meaning no one was on view, I'd bring my book bag and get started on my homework. But sometimes we were swamped with guests all night. Often people didn't want to leave at the close of business. It wasn't like we were at the mall and I could pull down the grates or make an announcement on the loudspeaker that we were about to shut down. Since I didn't have the heart to put someone out who was already in mourning, I just left my mother waiting inside her car with her doors locked, though I tried not to leave her waiting longer than fifteen minutes. Then I'd go stand in the viewing room with a stern face and crossed arms. When that didn't work, I'd start switching off the lights all the way in the back, and families usually got the picture.

On really slow nights, Mr. Wylie would come into the office and chat with me. The office was tangibly different since Brandon was away at school and Chanel had been fired. He'd let me ask him about anything and then he'd tell me all the gossip. I knew which funeral directors couldn't pay their bills, who had to go before the state board, and whose kids were flunking out of mortuary school. Because we had church in common, I was a good sounding board. In one breath he'd tell me about a church revival; in the next he'd tell me whose rent the church had to pay.

If we were in my office, he'd go over the cases that Ms. Angela worked on during the day to check for oversights, and then he'd hand them over to me for a final glance. If we were in his office, he signed off on checks as he talked and would give me notes of things I needed to complete the next day. He always updated me on Brandon's status in school. I spoke to him like a grown-up, and if I had been old enough, I probably would have lit a cigarette and smoked one with him while we talked, like Ms. Angela did. When he told me why he stopped talking to another director, I'd tell him that was silly or unchristian.

"Shucks," he'd say in response.

When I asked him if he would let Chanel come back if she wanted to, he softened and said she would always have a place at Wylie Funeral Home.

Maybe Brandon's absence made it easier for me to step in and become close to Mr. Wylie, but without even realizing it, I'd become his pupil. The funeral home was like a huge college campus for me to explore, and in his classroom an A was the only acceptable grade. If someone made a mistake, he would yell. If someone took too long completing a task, he'd holler. His forceful tongue scolded me when I was wrong, but he paid me well when I was right. I'd seen him fuss at a grown man so badly for not executing one of his directives on a service that the guy was driven to tears. Because he was a perfectionist, he made some of the men nervous, and because they were so anxious not to mess up, they ended up making mistakes. That's why I made it my business to get everything right the first time.

One Friday evening, Mr. Wylie cut our routine powwow rather short because there was a body in the house that needed his immediate attention. So he slipped upstairs to exchange his suave suit and tie for clothes he didn't mind trashing after the embalming procedure and headed downstairs. He called the embalming room the "prep room," but I always thought of it as an operating room. It was the heart of the funeral home, where human blood was sacrificed for a postmortem ceremony.

I was surfing the Internet when I heard his booming voice

through the intercom. "Helloooo!" That was how he called for us. I picked up right away. "I need you in the basement." *Click*. That was all he said.

I assumed that he was calling me down because there was a clerical task he needed me to do. I knew I couldn't leave him waiting like I had the casket guy, so I grabbed a pen and pad and headed down, trembling. I was about to come face-to-face with the ugly side of death's business.

As soon as I opened the door that led downstairs, the sound of gospel music drifted up to meet me. It sounded like a Baptist revival was taking place down there. I held on to the walls as I tiptoed down the steps, while each of my footsteps echoed back to me. It was like hearing my shadow.

I stopped at the bottom of the stairs about five feet from the closet where I had found the church truck. The darkened rooms that I had avoided before were now beaming bright. To my left was a doorway, which I refused to face. I had a photographic memory and surely whatever I saw would find a permanent space in my head. So I walked backward until my back was against the wall.

Then I called out to him. "Yes, Mr. Wylie."

All I wanted was to hear his voice, to know another living person was there with me. I had no intention of moving beyond the square tile where I was standing. I just wanted him to yell some instructions to me and send me back upstairs.

"You see the rag?" he hollered back to me.

"Mm-hm," I answered, never even turning my head in that direction.

"Wipe that casket down for me." His voice sounded muffled.

"Okay."

As simple as the assignment sounded, I could not focus on it because I was trying to wrap my mind around what could have been happening on the other side of the wall. I had been in the basement for at least four or five minutes and had not seen Mr. Wylie. It was a sure sign that he was deeply engrossed in his work.

Nevertheless, I mustered all my nerve and pushed my fear to the side. With my hand on the wall for stability, I pivoted into the dressing room. Fluorescent lights cast shadows over the silver minimum metal casket that was sitting atop a church truck in the center of the floor. I locked my eyes on it and hoped to keep them there for the duration of my stay. I could see where the dust had accumulated on the coffin, but I still didn't believe that it warranted my trip to the basement. After all the strides I'd made, this felt like a punishment of sorts. It felt like *Scared Straight*, the "Don't End Up in the Embalming Room" version. But deep down I also knew it was a privilege to be there, in Mr. Wylie's private sanctum.

"The rag is on the chair," Mr. Wylie called out from the adjoining room. I felt his movement but still had no inclination to look in his direction. I inched my way toward the chair, feeling blindly until the rag was in my hand.

My ears picked up the sounds coming from my left: the squish of Mr. Wylie's sneakers on the floor, water running from a faucet, metal clanking. I tried to tune them out and focus on the gospel music coming out of the speakers, but I couldn't.

"There's spray too," he instructed me.

"Okay." I wanted to say something more profound—make a joke or ask a question—but I just couldn't.

I grabbed the spray and squirted a light layer, taking care

to be gentle as I cleaned. I purposely avoided wiping the foot of the casket because I knew that everything going on behind me would come into view if I stood down there.

Part of me knew that the sooner I got this over with, the better. I understood that Mr. Wylie was lonely in the embalming room while Brandon was away, since Brandon used to keep him company while he worked. But in my mind, Mr. Wylie had the radio—Heaven 600, the spirit of gospel. He had the young man he was embalming. He was a deacon at the church. He had Jesus. He didn't need me to keep him company that night.

As I stood cleaning the casket, trying to concentrate on the task at hand, I began to take in my surroundings. The dressing room was a dead man's green room. It was where smiles were constructed, eyes were permanently glued shut, and the dead came to life. I felt like I had walked into a makeup artist's playground. On my left was an open cabinet with more makeup than a drag queen's vanity. Tubes of lipstick were strewn across the table in front of me, in shades of deep plum, ruby red, coral, and pink. Palettes of eye shadow and compacts of blush, foundation, and concealer were piled high.

On closer inspection, I realized that much of it was mortuary makeup, not the brands I coveted from the department stores. Instead there were jars of camouflage cream, translucent powders that were mixed with skin tones, lip tints used to create a natural lip color, and waxes that filled holes and wounds—the makeup Mr. Wylie used to create a facade of health for the families we serviced.

Three Styrofoam mannequin heads sat on a table. Two of them wore wigs. Older women whose hair had thinned or had become difficult to manage usually needed a wig for viewing. Sometimes a family might buy more than one, or Mr. Wylie would go out and select one that he thought looked better. A few extras were left in the dressing room. Almost every woman we buried needed her hair styled.

Styling a black woman's hair required special supplies. Mr. Wylie's selection was impressive, as if he'd learned from Madame C.J. Walker herself. The hair station was thoroughly equipped, like a full-fledged beauty salon. There was a jumbo jar of Pro Styl brown gel, which helped to slick down unruly tresses. He had Pump It Up, a toxic danger to your airway and the ozone layer that held a curl in place like no other. And oil sheen made it all shine! On an adjacent cart was a hot-curler stove and different-size barrel curlers. When it came to hair, Mr. Wylie mostly left it to the professionals. We had an on-call beautician come in whenever someone needed his or her hair done. Families were charged seventy-five dollars for this service.

Behind me stood three empty stainless steel tables with wheels shining like my grandmother's silver. These were the tables where Mr. Wylie dressed the bodies. Next to them were a few trash cans and a chair that was filled with newspaper and batting cotton, filler used under clothes to make them fit perfectly.

When I finished dusting the casket, I intended to slip out unscathed, but I caught a glimpse of Mr. Wylie through the connecting door. There, in plain sight, was Mr. Wylie with a mask over his face, standing over the body of a young boy and waving a wand-like tool, like he was conducting an orchestra. His hands were moving so quickly that my eyes could hardly keep up. An apron fit snugly around his waist. He looked like he had been doing this his entire life.

A white marble embalming table, as cold and stiff as its occupant, stood in the center of the room. The tools of Mr. Wylie's trade were spread neatly across the adjacent shelves. When Mr. Wylie moved from the head of the table, I saw a boy with his skull wide open, the spongy contents of his head pouring out. I was instantly flushed with fever and could feel a burning sensation all over my body, but I could not look away. So I stood beneath the fluorescent bulbs that shined light down on us and I let sweat pour from my palms. This was the one time I wished I had listened to my father.

The embalming room was extremely uncomfortable to be in. It was a dank, windowless chamber that let off a toxic odor I hadn't smelled when I was standing in the dressing room. It was strong enough to revive the faint. In a room so white—white walls, white tables, white floors, and white ceiling tiles—I felt like I needed a straitjacket. The open cabinet on the right added a splash of color with its different colored bottles of cavity, the high-powered formaldehyde used to preserve the organs in the body. The colors varied, depending on which company they came from and the strength of the chemicals. Some bottles were white; others were green, pink, or orange. It took an experienced embalmer to know which fluids were needed for a particular case—a person's size or type of illness could determine the strength of the fluid you'd need. Also in the cabinet were pre-injection chemicals that broke up clots and conditioned vessels to make the embalming process flow smoothly.

A clean sink stood to the left, where Mr. Wylie washed his hands after embalming, while the drain at the foot of the embalming table washed away everything else. In front of the embalming table was a big machine that was bubbling with an orange fluid. A five-gallon tank with knobs on the bottom, it looked like a gigantic blender. The tube attached to it was in Mr. Wylie's hand.

"Just look at this." He shook his head and sighed in disgust. He waited for me to move closer. Then he lifted the dead boy's forearm with his free hand. A well-crafted suicide note was etched into the boy's skin: "I want Peanut to cut my hair and my eyes open," it said. He had carefully traced the letters in each word deep into his flesh so that they stood out boldly. These were his last wishes, directives for his funeral. Peanut must've been his barber, and he wanted his eyes left wide open during his service.

One year older than me, this boy had ended it all with a self-inflicted gunshot wound. With soap and a washrag and his hands stuffed inside latex gloves, Mr. Wylie scrubbed the boy's forearm hard, the same way my mother once scrubbed permanent marker from my arms, rubbing and rubbing until the ink disappeared and the evidence of his sins no longer existed. I stood far enough away so that I would not be splashed with any of the liquids and watched the mixture of blood and water, which looked like pink lemonade, as it flowed down the drain. I wasn't wearing anything to protect me like Mr. Wylie was, and I didn't want to be marked by the moment. But it didn't matter. Everything I saw that night was already etched into my mind, leaving a permanent stain.

I watched as the young boy's body surrendered to Mr. Wylie's ministrations, following his every command. His body lay faceup, his hands at his sides. Mr. Wylie's methodical style weaved repetition and rhythm with precision and skill.

"Can you believe this?" Mr. Wylie went on.

Among the boy's belongings was a photo of a young woman. Mr. Wylie passed the photo to me. The girl was quite attractive, a little thick, but attractive.

"Just stupid," he said.

"Who's this?" I asked, looking for the story behind the suicide.

"His giiirrl," he said in a teasing way.

"But wait. Are you going to let Peanut cut his hair and leave his eyes open?"

"Noooooo! When you go back upstairs, page Cidney the Barber and see if she will come in the morning to cut his hair." He had already scrubbed the boy's entire body and cleaned his nails. By tomorrow the boy's head would be put back together again, and Mr. Wylie would have our beautician come and trim his hair.

I sympathized with the young boy, but I wanted to yell. I wanted to shake him back to life. In that moment, I didn't want to be there. I wanted to be a hotline operator with words that encouraged him while he was still alive. I wanted arms strong enough to hold him until the urge for him to end his life surrendered to my embrace.

The boy was naked, but I was too ashamed to look at his privates. Mr. Wylie had already removed the sutures that held together the Y incision made earlier by the medical examiner. I would later learn that an incision was made from each shoulder to the middle of the chest and then down to the pubic bone during a typical autopsy. For a woman, the incision would have gone around her breasts and met in the middle of her chest. In the case of this boy, on account of his gunshot wound to the head, an incision had also been made in his head, and parts had been removed. That's why I was staring at his open skull.

When a body was autopsied by the medical examiner—as in this case—the organs were removed for examination and studied to determine a cause of death. The viscera, as they are called, were then placed inside a plastic bag. Those organs still needed to be treated—embalmed. So Mr. Wylie poured two bottles of cavity into the bag containing the boy's viscera, as well as three scoops of the white embalming powder. The mix was strong and burned my eyes a bit. Then he shook the bag a little before he tied it off with a double seal. He placed it to the side until the end of the embalming process.

One bottle of the liquid cavity fluid was used during the first embalming. During this time blood and fluid were sucked out of the body in a process called aspirating. This suction is an important part of the embalming process because a person's lungs can still have fluid, the heart can still contain blood, and the intestines mostly are still holding feces after death. Cavity is then put into those areas to help firm and preserve. After eight hours, or in this case on the following day, Mr. Wylie would come back and re-aspirate the body, then inject another half bottle of fluid.

I watched Mr. Wylie place the arterial tube into the boy's body and inject him with the embalming fluid. Because the boy's heart was in the bag with the rest of the organs, a vascular injection couldn't be made. Not everyone is autopsied, so in a normal embalming the blood is drained from the jugular or femoral vein and disinfecting fluid is injected through the femoral artery. If there had not been an autopsy, Mr. Wylie would have aspirated fluids out of the body cavity by making a small incision near the navel.

Though the humming of the Duotronic pump machine had to compete with the church announcements on Heaven 600, I could clearly hear the suction and bubbly swooshing of the fluids. As the machine ran, Mr. Wylie began to massage the boy's legs. He explained that he was looking for firmness or goose bumps to see how well the process was working. He wanted the legs to fill out and the skin to fall back into place. He worked his way up, rubbing the arms, underarms, and hands. He even massaged the boy's face and neck.

A filler had to be used to fill up the cavity. Then the viscera were placed back inside the body. Finally, Mr. Wylie sutured the body and the cranium. Once the embalming was finished, he washed the boy's body down again.

Embalming isn't just about preservation; it is also about disinfecting, about purifying the body. It is as much a ritual in restoration as it is a costly procedure that is necessary for those who wish to have a body present during a eulogy. Mr. Wylie had done this hundreds, if not thousands, of times.

As much as I hated watching the embalming process, I would eventually come to understand that it was just as important as anything else I'd ever learn in the business, if not more. The ancient art of embalming was the reason funeral homes even existed. While we use the practice to preserve bodies for viewings and funerals, the Egyptians had something totally different in mind when they invented it. For them, mummification was a way of readying a physical body so that the soul could return to the preserved corpse. For us, it buys us time to visit our loved ones without decomposition, maggots, or odors.

Now embalming is what keeps funeral directors in business. While law does not require it, millions of families choose the procedure because it provides closure. But some Jews and Muslims consider the practice a desecration of the body and avoid it by burying a body within forty-eight hours of death.

For the few Muslim services we did, the process of prepping a body was much different. The imam would bring members of the masjid along and they would pray together in Arabic in a sacred ceremony in the basement while washing the body down. This was the only time Mr. Wylie allowed outsiders in his prep room. After methodically bathing the body, they would wrap it in a white sheet and return to the masjid for a brief service that involved a closed casket. Since the actual casket wouldn't be buried, we would loan the mourners a blue dinghy to transport the body. After the service, Mr. Wylie would lead the family to the cemetery, where members of the masjid would remove the wrapped body from the casket and cast it back into the earth, creating a freshly dug grave for flesh and bone.

• • • •

AFTER I'd seen Mr. Wylie work a few more times in the basement, the beauty of the process began to captivate me. When I told Mr. Wylie about my interest, he quickly shut me down.

"Nah, you're too smart for this. Be a doctor."

CHAPTER
SEVEN

MY parents weren't interested in my stories from the basement, so I told the one girl at school who would listen, Tuverla Jones. She wasn't in any of my classes, but I saw her before and after school and would share the gruesome details. The first time I told her I worked at a funeral home, she was mesmerized. She was adamant that she wanted to become a mortician when she graduated. She already looked the part, so when she told me that this was her future goal, I believed her. Her lips were always lined in black lip liner and her ponytail was stacked high on her head. She wore dark colors too. Her face was always so serious for someone who was just in high school. I tried to tell her about all the other positions there were in the funeral business, but she made it clear that she wanted to embalm bodies. Other than Tuverla, no one else wanted to hear about the embalming.

But that didn't mean they weren't curious about my world.

Every time I told someone I worked at the funeral home, they'd ask the same questions: Had I ever witnessed a corpse exhale for the last time? Had I ever seen a body sit up? Had one jumped on me? Had we ever embalmed someone who wasn't really dead? I knew those questions would sound ridiculous to Mr. Wylie, but I too was haunted by the image of a corpse springing to life or taking a final breath right in front of me. So I pretended to ask on behalf of the people who asked me. If I was going to spend time in the basement, I needed to know what I was in for.

I waited until I had been in the basement a few more times before I worked up the courage. As soon as the opportunity presented itself, I became relentless with the questioning. I was worse than a three-year-old.

"Can I ask you a question?"

"Go on." While Mr. Wylie's patience usually ran thin with others, he didn't have a problem with my questions. No matter how absurd they were, he'd take a deep breath and a long pause and then give me his most honest answer.

"Does a body take a last breath?" As soon as the words left my lips, I knew they sounded silly. But Mr. Wylie paused and explained patiently that the idea was just folklore that continued to resurrect itself from generation to generation. He said the human body is filled with different fluids and gases, but he assured me that I never had to worry about a body gasping for air while I was in the basement.

"Well, what about a body jumping? Does that ever happen?" I continued my questioning.

"Yeah, when some jackleg mortician injects too much embalming fluid, the body may react," he said indignantly.

"Jackleg" was a term we heard almost daily. This was the word he used for anyone he thought was incompetent, which was virtually everyone in the green book. "Call the jackleg plumber," he would instruct me at times. Or if our organist was unavailable for a service he'd say, "Get me the jackleg musician." It seemed like everyone was a jackleg, so I was confused by whom he was referring to most of the time.

"Really?" I knew it was silly, but I was relieved. It was then that I really accepted that the morticians were the puppeteers pulling all the strings. They were the minds behind the body, and there wasn't an angry soul in the corpse to fear.

"Yeah, the muscles might spasm and cause the body to have a movement," he explained.

"Oh, okay." Since he wasn't a jackleg mortician, we had nothing to worry about.

• • • •

ONCE I crossed the threshold for the first time, Mr. Wylie's sanctuary, the basement, became my playground. With all the crazies coming in and out on the floors above, sometimes the basement seemed like the safest place. When I wasn't there, it was all I could think about. The thrill did not fade. The colors. The movement. Everything was so rhythmic. The innate sense of precision Mr. Wylie used to aspirate and re-aspirate, removing another man's blood and injecting him with a final dose of life. When I looked at my hands, I couldn't envision them inside another body. They were too shaky to suture, too chubby for precision. I still squirmed when I saw an open wound.

But I could still hear the whoosh of the chemicals and the clinking sound of his tools hitting the table. It all fascinated me. Whenever I entered, I left the rest of the world behind me. It felt like time stopped when I was in the basement.

I came to understand the peace of the embalming room. It is a place of transition between this world and the heavens, profound and serene. I imagined angels talking to the bodies and reassuring them as the gatekeeper in the sky waited for their souls to arrive.

On days when we weren't busy, Mr. Wylie would invite me down. I'd bring my pen and pad because he usually had a list of tasks to call off to me. "Order Ms. Such and Such a nameplate. Tell Ms. Avalon to come do this head tomorrow. Get me a blue dinghy." After he finished his list, I'd stand in the doorway and watch him embalm and dress and casket. Sometimes he needed a hand and I would help him lift a body or polish fingernails. I felt like his apprentice. Dozens of girls would have loved to have filled my shoes and worked under his tutelage. I had the résumés on my desk to prove it, but I knew how many of them never made it past the first interview. I felt privileged that he let me into his world.

As we talked in the basement, I heard Mr. Wylie's loneliness trapped in his throat. It was the reality of living in an empty house with dead bodies for company, of longing to be surrounded by family.

I was also struggling with loneliness. My house still felt empty without Aunt Mary, my parents were consumed with work and church and serving on boards, and my sister was away at college. I could never replace Brandon for Mr. Wylie, nor he Aunt Mary for me, but for the time being we both filled a void.

In those quiet afternoons we had together, I learned that the secrets of the trade are complex and not obvious to the average eye. Turn your head for a second, and you'll miss the tip of a tie being snipped to make a pocket piece or batting cotton being tucked beneath a man's shirt to fill out his suit.

I was shocked when I saw one of the most common tricks in the book. One afternoon I walked in as Mr. Wylie was dressing a man. He had already gotten him into his undershirt, boxers, socks, pants, and shirt, all of the garments that we required. Shoes weren't necessary unless there was going to be a full couch—a casket with both ends opened. All the man needed was his tie and suit jacket and he was ready to be casketed. But I couldn't believe what Mr. Wylie did next. He took a pair of scissors and slit the man's suit jacket up the back. This is a technique that directors sometimes use to protect the outer layer of clothing from being damaged. I thought he had gone mad to destroy such an expensive coat, but then I watched him take one side and pull the man's arm through and then do the same with the other side. He smoothed the jacket down the front and fastened the buttons, then tucked the extra material under the torso so you would never know it had been cut at all. This was the technique he used when dressing most men.

When people chose the outfit their loved ones would be buried in, they never considered weight loss or weight gain. The clothes that someone wore a month before becoming ill or being placed on a ventilator (which can cause fluid retention), would often not fit quite right. In the afterlife, you no longer had the luxury of greasing yourself down or sucking in your belly to get into a pair of jeans. But Mr. Wylie would try his best to get you in, even if it meant becoming a makeshift tailor.

We had a few close calls when it came to fitting clothes. Mr. Wylie usually had a very good eye for men's sizes and could guide a family on what size clothes they'd need to bring or buy just by looking at the body. But there was a time when he miscalculated and cut a jacket that was too small for a man in the arms. The jacket was destroyed, and since it was our mistake, Mr. Wylie had to send Ms. Angela to Macy's to find a replica. Luckily, it turned out replacing the navy suit jacket was easier than we had expected.

That wasn't the case when we dressed a biker who had died tragically on his motorcycle and whose family wanted to honor him by burying him in his motorcycle uniform. He was a pretty hefty boy and the fluid from the life support machine had caused his body to swell, so he just wasn't going to be able to fit into the unstretchable leather jacket that he used to wear. But Mr. Wylie's assistant didn't catch the problem, so he took a pair of shears to the jacket, cutting about an inch up the back before Mr. Wylie could stop him. There was no way we would ever find a duplicate jacket, so Mr. Wylie had to call the family and ask them to go out to buy a new jacket two sizes larger.

Wardrobe malfunctions that were our fault were a rarity, though. The real dressing issues were a matter of downright decency. Some families couldn't afford to buy new clothes for a funeral or just believed that they shouldn't let a good suit go to waste. Sometimes these families brought us clothes with visible stains or even a filthy stench clinging to them. Occasionally, the clothes were so dirty that Mr. Wylie sent them out to the dry cleaner at his own expense. He even donated ties from his personal collection to families who really needed them.

I was often responsible for receiving the clothes when a

family dropped them off, and I would have to go through the entire bag of garments to ensure that we had everything we needed before the family member left. People could be buried in whatever their family chose for them to wear; however, there was one exception to the rule. All tops had to have long sleeves. If someone had been in the hospital before death, he or she had probably had an IV, which sometimes left ugly bruises that were hard to cover. The wounds could cause leakage, and we often needed to wrap arms in batting cotton to prevent a mess. Although not all cases had been treated with an IV, it just made it easier when making arrangements to request long-sleeve shirts from families as a matter of course.

For the most part, I was neutral when it came to fashion choices, but my pet peeve was when families wouldn't splurge on new underwear. I understood that bras were expensive, and underwear, especially men's, usually came in a pack and no one wanted to be stuck with three extra pairs of boxers that probably would get no use. But on too many occasions loved ones brought in old panties and raggedy bras. I just thought that everyone should be wearing new undies when they went to heaven, or at least clean ones.

While there were some undergarments that didn't make the cut, there were others that were over the top for the afterlife. The sexiest underwear we received was for an eighteen-year-old transvestite named Vicki, who had been born as Anthony Taylor. Vicki had died from AIDS, and before her death she had been taking hormones to begin her transition to becoming a woman.

One afternoon, a black woman and a white woman who were Vicki's friends greeted me at the door to make funeral arrangements for the friend they called Anthony. I walked them into the arrangement room and sat them across the table from me. As usual, I began to ask for the personal information that was needed for the green card.

"What's the correct spelling of his name?" I asked.

"A-n-t-h-o-n-y." The white woman, Mary, spelled out his name, enunciating every syllable. Then I asked for his address.

I continued my questions. Marital status: single. Citizen: USA. Then in the middle of my Q and A, somewhere in between parents' names and occupation, they broke in and asked, "Excuse me. Who's going to do her hair?" The black woman sitting across from me, Gina, seemed really concerned.

"I'm sorry? Her who?" I asked, completely confused since we were talking about Anthony.

"Well she's transgendered. She lived as a woman," said Mary

"Never mind. We'll bring a wig," Gina interjected.

"She went by Vicki," Mary explained.

I tried not to look surprised, but I'm sure my facial expression gave me away. We had never had a case like this before. Before I moved on to the next question, I realized suddenly that the black woman sitting across from me was also transgendered. Her weave hung past her shoulders, and she was wearing tight blue jeans and a shirt that bared her midriff. I had admired her body as I escorted her down to the arrangement room, but now I was reexamining everything. From what I could see, Mary was all woman. I later learned that she worked with transgendered people to help them through their process.

I pulled out the items-needed form to complete.

"Will she be dressed as a man or woman?" I felt ridiculous asking, but I had to know for sure.

"A woman, of course."

I completed the form we used to record how the deceased would be dressed, only instead of writing "suit, tie, shirt," I wrote that we'd need a long-sleeve blouse and skirt or pants, or a dress, and a bra, panties, and a full slip. The next business day they brought me her clothes. Usually a simple process, this time it became an elaborate fashion consultation. Inside the bag was a black lace push-up bra, a sexy thong, a pair of skin-tight black jeans, and a short black lace blouse. I had never ever seen anyone buried in a thong before.

"She had breasts before she got sick. Can you pad it for her?" said Mary.

"No problem," I responded.

Since Vicki's breasts hadn't fully developed, she could only fill an A cup, but her friend pulled me aside and asked if we could boost her cup size up to a B by stuffing her bra.

The photos we had seen showed that Vicki was gorgeous before her sickness began eating away at her. Her face was tender, her manly features disguised beneath makeup. She looked as if she was born to be a woman. I'm sure she fooled many straight men into buying her a drink. Yet on the dressing table, with no makeup, she looked like a little boy who had been playing in his mother's wig collection. And from where I was standing, Vicki couldn't hide that she was packing. But I could also see that her breasts had begun to bud, just as Mary had said.

Mr. Wylie's helpers were uncomfortable about dressing Vicki like a woman when she was clearly a man, but they honored her friends' request and stuffed her bra with batting cotton, removed the glued-in tracks of her weave from her hair, and replaced them with a wig. She looked perfect.

Vicki was laid out on the floor for viewing in a blue dinghy because technically she was a social service case and her friends were still having issues with the finances. There were a few floral arrangements in the room, but not many.

Gina and Mary arrived first. Still dressed in sexy, form-fitting clothes, they stopped at the register stand to sign in for the viewing. Gina looked up at the marquee, which had a photo of Vicki and a listing of her funeral arrangements. When I made the marquee, I typed Vicki's given name—Anthony Taylor—as a matter of course, since I had used that name for all the other documents.

"Take it down! Take it down now! Oh my God," Gina was screaming at me.

"Do you have some Wite-Out or something?" she yelled.

I took the marquee out of the holder and brought it up-stairs to the office, where I quickly made a new one that simply read "Vicki"—no last name. I brought it down and handed it to Vicki's friend, who was pleased. I walked the women into the viewing room, where they made a fuss over Vicki.

After a few moments I heard one of them say, "Girl, she looks good. And look at those boobies."

The rest of the guests were waiting outside to view her body. Vicki was part of the Revlon Family, a group of trans-gendered and homosexual individuals in Baltimore who had formed the tight-knit family structure to support one another. According to Vicki Revlon's survivors list in her funeral pro-gram, she was leaving to mourn her "Revlon mother and fa-ther," her "Revlon siblings," and a host of "cousins," "aunts," and "uncles," and even a "daughter" in the group. Her real family members were not mentioned in the obituary.

I stood by the front door, fascinated by them, trying to figure out who was who. Every woman who walked in that afternoon had in fact been born a man, but you'd never know it. They had gorgeous faces with immaculate makeup. Hair weaves that made Janet Jackson's look shabby. A few had huge breasts.

As they strutted up the stairs to the building, I tried not to stare, but I was amazed and a little envious of their striking beauty. Despite the huge hands and awkward feet, they looked perfect. Some were fixing their makeup, while others were crying. I'd never seen so many divas in one place all at once.

There was also a group of guys there to see Vicki, who I assumed were her Revlon brothers. One guy was wearing a pair of baggy jeans, sneakers, and a polo shirt. I thought he was cute until I looked down and noticed that he was developing breasts and had probably been taking hormones like Vicki.

• • • •

COSMETICS were the most important part of the prepping process. The whole purpose of a viewing is to have one last look at the face of a loved one, one last memory. Mr. Wylie understood this and took his time with every case. Many families didn't understand that when he asked for a photo, he used it as a guide for his work, so they would bring in photos of a sixty-year-old man in his youth, or a side profile, or some other picture that would not be helpful for him when he tried to restore a person's true features. Sometimes Mr. Wylie would have to request a more recent picture, and he accepted anything: a driver's license, a passport, a tarnished Polaroid, whatever he could get.

We once had a daughter come in to view her father. Her dad had been terminally ill for about a year before he died, and she'd spent every day nursing him. The daughter had brought in a photograph that had been taken right before his sickness got the best of him. Mr. Wylie filled out his face, which had become very thin and sunken, as it was pictured. The old man's skin was a little darker than the photo because of his illness, but there wasn't much Mr. Wylie could do to lighten the complexion.

When his daughter came in, she stood before the casket for a few moments, inspecting everything, and then she walked around and read the notes on the cards before circling back and pausing again in front of the casket. Then she burst into tears. "He doesn't look dead enough. I don't like it. He looks too healthy."

After she and Mr. Wylie discussed the issue, she admitted that the photo she'd given us was more than two years old. She had become used to her father's dying face and wanted to remember him as the sick man that she had cared for and known most recently. Mr. Wylie agreed to make changes. He knew you only got one chance at funeral service and he was happy he could honor a family's request, no matter how strange it seemed.

After ushering the family out of the room and pulling the curtains shut, he went to the casket and began massaging the area around the man's cheekbones with his thumb and index finger. He added pressure and pushed the skin in, making the man's face look thinner. The more he rubbed, the more the man's face sunk in, removing the man's youth before my eyes, and adding a look of death. But that was exactly what the daughter wanted. She returned, and when she saw her father again, she gave Mr. Wylie a hug.

• • • •

MR. Wylie had given me some important assignments in the basement, and I'd had no problem earning my stripes. I had lifted a man's legs and helped slide him down into a casket. I had pin curled a woman's hair, filed and painted fingernails, and helped shake out wigs. I'd even become an ad hoc stylist on occasion. Once, Mr. Wylie needed to prepare a woman who had very thin hair on the top of her scalp. The family refused to buy a wig because they had become used to seeing their mother with thin, hot combed hairstyle as she'd always worn it. So Mr. Wylie fired up the marcel, a little stove used by professional beauticians to heat curling irons, and stuck the hot combs inside until they were hot enough to straighten her hair. When he tried to style the poor little lady's hair, though, he gave her lopsided bangs. I snipped half a centimeter off and curled and feathered the bangs. Her family said they hadn't seen her look that good in years.

All these tasks were minuscule, however, compared to what he asked me to do in a case that was one of the toughest I had.

I knew there was a baby in the house before Mr. Wylie called me downstairs, because the folder on Ms. Angela's desk had the sickening word "baby" in front of the deceased's name and the year of birth and death were the same. I knew I didn't want to be involved in the case. I didn't want to help this time. "They're in a better place now," or "It's just a body," I'd usually tell myself before I worked on bodies with Mr. Wylie. But I knew that the way I usually reconciled my feelings about our cases might not cut it this time.

However, I knew what I had to do. In the basement, I found Mr. Wylie working on an older woman. Relieved that the baby wasn't in sight, I hovered in the doorway close enough to answer the phone in the dressing room by the second ring. Mr. Wylie always said the phone in the embalming room was "too nasty" for me to use, and looking at all the stains on his smock, I was glad that it was still off limits.

"You see those clothes on that hook?" He talked to me as he was preparing the woman.

"Yes." A white satin three-piece set that was small enough to fit a Cabbage Patch doll hung on the wall of the dressing room.

"You're going to dress that baby," he said, pointing to the table in the dressing room.

"I'm going to dress that baby?" I had been standing next to the small child the entire time but hadn't noticed since the body was tucked beneath a white sheet and just looked like a tiny lump. Since I was so used to seeing adults openly displayed on that table, I couldn't help but imagine that the poor baby was in bad condition if Mr. Wylie had kept it hidden. I hadn't seen the baby's death certificate, so I didn't know what had happened.

The fact that babies are so fragile had always made me nervous around them. I never wanted to hold my newborn little cousins because I feared that I would hurt them. I knew there was a certain way to rest their tiny heads, and I was clumsy and sometimes too rough. And though this baby couldn't suffer anymore, it still looked so vulnerable.

An autopsy had been performed by the medical examiner's office, and when I lifted the cloth, I could see that the baby had sutures holding him together. He wasn't even six months old, but you could tell he had been eating well. His chubby cheeks looked like they had been stained a deep purple, but otherwise he just looked like a beautiful sleeping infant on the outside, with an innocence on his face that covered it like a mask. A crown of curls rested on his head, and his ten tiny toes and fingers were perfectly made. There were no signs of trauma or abuse. I imagined he was dreaming of sugarplum fairies.

Earlier that day his mother, with two eyes full of tears and two breasts still full of milk, had dropped his clothes off and asked how her baby looked. "Like an angel," I had replied without any thought. What else do you tell a mother at that moment? When she embraced me, I knew I had said the right thing.

"Get that Pamper over there," Mr. Wylie instructed me.

Pamper, I thought. I guess it made sense. Adult women needed a bra, panties, a full slip, and panty hose. And adult men needed socks, underpants, and an undershirt. I guess a baby needed something to cover his bottom as well. I took the Pamper and unfolded it very carefully. I lifted the baby's bottom and dragged the diaper underneath, and then securely taped each side.

"Look!" I held the baby out toward Mr. Wylie as if he was a new dad. "Did I do this right?"

Mr. Wylie poked his head in the dressing room. "Good.

Now take his undershirt and put it on," he yelled as he continued re-aspirating the body on the embalming table.

"It's called a onesie, you know?"

"I don't care what it is called. You got it on yet?"

I lifted the shirt over the baby's head and tugged his tiny
arms through the sleeves. Then I smoothed out the one-piece
undershirt and snapped it between his legs. I took the cute cro-
cheted booties from the bag his mother had left, and I put them
on his feet and then carefully dressed him in a formal shirt, satin
suit, and suspenders. The finishing touch was a matching sweater.
He looked sharp, like he was on his way to be christened. Still, I
didn't know how to feel about dressing a baby. I couldn't understand why he was even here. He'd never had a chance to live.

Mr. Wylie looked in and gave his nod of approval.

"Get the oil sheen," Mr. Wylie instructed, barely looking
up from the body he was working on. I had seen him spray the
hair product on the faces of other bodies just before taking
them upstairs to put on view, so I sprayed a little on the baby's
face to give him a shimmering glow. Now there was truth to
what I'd told his mother earlier. He looked heavenly.

Mr. Wylie had ordered a small white cherub casket a few
days earlier, about twenty inches in length, small enough for
me to carry in my arms. I placed him in the tiny burial container and Mr. Wylie came in and gave the baby a final look.
"You did good," he said while he shook my hand. Then he
smoothed the baby's clothes until they were perfect and sent
me upstairs to get one of the singing teddy bears for the casket.
The baby was ready for viewing and I had officially dressed my
first body on my own, which was a very big deal.

Babies became my weak spot. The longer I worked at the funeral home, the more I'd try to convince myself that there was a greater purpose in death—that it held meaning for those left behind, a profound message on how to live the life they still had on this earth. But the baby cases shook the neat understanding I'd created. There was nothing to learn from them. If the good die young, then a baby was a saint.

• • • •

IN two years I had proven myself to be an important part of Mr. Wylie's business. At the end of the month, I coded all the checks for his accountant, which gave me insight into where every dime of his money went. I also sent out personal thank-you cards to the families we'd served during the month. But while I thought there was complete transparency when it came to me and Mr. Wylie, there was one little detail that he kept under wraps from us all—he was planning a secret wedding.

I knew her only as the voice on the phone. She was the woman that he stopped everything for. If he was embalming, he wanted her call. If he was on a service, you'd better page him to let him know she rang. Whenever she called, she asked to speak to "Mr. Wylie." She never called him by his first name, and when someone asked who was speaking, she would always say "Ms. McFadden." I remember Chanel disliking her for that reason. "Ms. McFadden. *Hmph!* Your name is Charleen. We all know who you are."

I had seen Ms. McFadden only once or twice in passing. She was twelve years Mr. Wylie's junior and wore bedazzled suits, the kind with shoulder pads decorated with sequins or rhinestones. Her hair was coiffed into a flawless bob back then. I'm sure Mr. Wylie footed the tab for her fancy wardrobe, since he thought a person's appearance was very important. When he hired a new apprentice, he gave him or her money to buy two brand-new suits from Macy's. He had his own manicurist come in and give him a manicure and pedicure. He used to give his second wife money to go shopping, but she'd come back with one item and keep the stack of cash. Money was no object when it came to his son and his woman.

On Valentine's Day, Mr. Wylie wed Ms. McFadden in a private ceremony at our church, with only his best friend and the mother of the bride in attendance. We never had even a clue about his plans, which was unusual since he couldn't keep a secret, so Ms. Angela and I were in complete shock when we learned there was a new Mrs. Wylie who would enter our world. We were even more surprised that Mr. Wylie hadn't even told Brandon, who was still away at school at the time. Maybe he feared it was too soon after his divorce, or maybe he just didn't want to jinx his third marriage by spreading the news.

A few days later, Ms. McFadden and her ten-year-old daughter moved into the third floor of the funeral home, which she intended to be only a temporary stop, since rumor had it that she had made it perfectly clear to Mr. Wylie before she married him that she wanted a home in the six-figure range. It took her a while to get used to her new living arrangement. One afternoon, she decided she wanted to fry chicken for dinner, which would have been fine except that we had a viewing going on downstairs, with a room full of guests. She lit the stove and dipped her flour-coated chicken into hot oil. Within minutes, the entire building smelled like a carryout. The visitors began to ask where the smell was coming from, and Mr. Wylie was not happy, but he loved his wife and told her she could eat out on days when viewings were scheduled.

I immediately clicked with the new Mrs. Wylie. Before she became a member of our church, she invited me to go to church with her and her daughter, and sometimes I would join her and Mr. Wylie for Sunday dinner. When her daughter began competing in beauty pageants, I went with them to the competitions. We were doing things as a family, and they also became a part of my family. When we had a party for New Year's Eve, my mother's birthday, or an anniversary, the Wylies were right there. I began calling them my godparents. When my parents went on vacation and didn't want me to be alone, I opted to stay with the Wylies.

I loved the way things were, but I knew Brandon would be graduating later that year. I wondered whether I'd still be such an important part of the Wylie family and business when he came home.

CHAPTER
EIGHT

THERE was always an air of anticipation on the morning of a service. The Cadillac hearse would sit alone in front of the funeral home, freshly buffed and shining. The day before, Mr. Wylie would assign Pork Chop, the neighborhood handyman, to soap the cars down until every visible particle had disappeared beneath his rag and he could see his chin hairs up close—through a door, rim, or glass. In this business, the cars were important. A symbol of status, a director's fleet needed to complement his swag. Mr. Wylie cared for his cars meticulously, leasing them so he'd always have the newest model. On the morning of a service, a funeral director would line up his luxury vehicles out front, so that everyone who passed by could admire the set of Lincolns or Cadillacs he kept pristine enough to chauffeur royalty. Families paid two hundred dollars for a hearse and another two hundred per limo, so they needed to be spotless. A seat in the limousine was a highly coveted position, since there were only seven to fight over. Usually, they'd go to the closest family members, or to the family elders out of respect, or to the person who took care of the deceased in his or her last hours. At the end of the day, though, the family member who footed the funeral bill decided who rode in the family car.

Mr. Wylie admitted that the cars were what attracted him to the funeral business in the first place. Every director that he'd ever seen drove a big fat Cadillac or Lincoln Town Car, donned fancy suits, and hadn't done anything illegal to earn them. Becoming a mortician was an attainable career goal that didn't require years and years of college but produced the same caliber professional. It bred entrepreneurs and businessmen who had a skill set similar to that of doctors, and legal knowledge that lawyers have.

Since funeral services were such a major event, sometimes it felt as though we were event planners. We helped to choose the venue: "How many guests are you expecting?" We booked the entertainment: "Do you have your own minister? Musician? Soloist?" We picked the decorations: "You're ordering a silver casket. Okay, we will have a silver nameplate and white hand bouquet ready." Then we had our glam squad, which consisted of wardrobe, hair, and makeup.

We were always on a tight schedule; we usually had less than a week to execute the game plan. As soon as the family walked out of the arrangement room we were already putting things in motion. Ms. Angela was on the phone verifying insurance policies. I was on another line booking an organist or preacher. And Mr. Wylie was on his cell phone telling Pork Chop when he needed the cars spic-and-span. All we needed was a down payment and we were all yours for the next three to seven days, however long it took to get your loved one buried. If a service took place seven days after the date of death, more than likely the family had financial or travel issues, or the person was a veteran or veteran's spouse and the veterans' cemetery was booked. The veterans' cemetery did a certain number of services a day, and once all a day's time slots were booked, you had to wait for the next available time.

The streets outside the funeral home would be lined with orange cones to reserve space for the cars that followed Mr. Wylie in the funeral procession, fresh off the prayer that he'd give before leaving the family's home. His prayers were so powerful, they often seemed like a mini-eulogy, and afterward the slow parade of vehicles, with flashing hazard lights and orange funeral tags stuck to the windshields, would make its way slowly down the block.

I'd wait with the body, which would already be lying "in state," a term used to describe when a body was set up for service. Setting up a body for a Saturday service would begin the night before. Before I closed down the funeral home at night, I'd cover the face of the person on view with a handkerchief: lacy cloth for women and plain for men. We always kept them covered out of respect and because Mr. Wylie's work needed to be in perfect condition the following day. In the morning, Mr. Wylie would remove the handkerchief and do a thorough inspection of the body, checking for leaks, smoothing the clothes, and touching up makeup wherever necessary. He'd switch on the casket lamps at the head and foot of the casket, and then finally illuminate the fixture attached to the hood of the casket, which beamed down like a spotlight.

Our chapel seated seventy-five comfortably, one hundred uncomfortably, and one hundred and fifty fire-hazardously, which we tried to avoid by offering the use of neighborhood churches if the event was going to be big. On our block there was Harlem Park Community Baptist Church, which had been a movie theater before it became a sanctuary. Diagonal to us was Unity United Methodist, a historic church. Both churches rented their facilities to us for funerals for two hundred and fifty dollars, which was the price we charged families. While the majority of our services were for traditional Christians, we did sometimes bury people with other beliefs. We never had a Jewish ceremony, but Muslims and Jehovah's Witnesses occasionally used us. Unlike Muslims, who didn't hold viewings and would have their services at the masjid, Jehovah's Witnesses usually held their services at the Kingdom Hall, their place of worship, but viewings were still held at our funeral home. When we held these viewings, we had to remove all traces of Christianity from our chapel, including the huge cross that stood in the center of the room.

If the service was in our chapel, I was charged with making sure that there was a box of tissues on hand and that the chapel temperature was neither too hot nor too cold. I'd roll the podium to the center of the floor and test the microphone with a "Helloooo," imitating Mr. Wylie. I'd put a stack of pens on the register stand and turn to a clean page in the book for people to acknowledge their attendance. With the high tide of emotions that rolled through a viewing, it was easy for families not to notice a visitor's presence.

At the service, I'd make sure there were no hiccups. Sometimes this meant guarding the family's seats. The first two rows were always reserved for immediate family, but without fail, someone else tried to sit there. I hated confrontation and never wanted to act like a drill sergeant; however, I had a responsibility to the family we were serving to make sure everything ran smoothly. Making sure some random cousin they probably hadn't seen in five years wasn't sitting in the VIP section when they arrived was just part of my job.

There was always someone who mixed up the funeral time and arrived hours before or after the service. Others purposely arrived early or late to avoid interacting with the family. This usually included estranged siblings, mistresses, folks who owed money to someone attending the funeral, or from what I overheard on different occasions, even the actual killer of the person in the casket. They would just sneak in, take a final look, and dash out.

• • • •

MR. Stan Bufford was our on-call organist. He could seduce the keys of Mr. Wylie's out-of-tune, ancient organ and create the most exhilarating melodies, and his captivating voice was just what I imagined angels would sound like as they ushered souls to heaven. He could hit the highest falsetto soprano note and then the lowest tenor note all in one verse. It was not uncommon for people to get whiplash because they turned their heads so fast to see if the person singing was a man or a woman, and they were always astonished not to see a heavyset old lady.

His Afro lay neatly on top of his head, perfectly cropped and oiled, accenting his pear-shaped face, and his cheeks puffed like a blowfish when he sang.

Families would always request him by saying, "We want the one who sounds like a woman." He could make a church hymn sound like a lullaby, making grown men cry and healthy women faint, grandmothers hum and babies fall asleep. When a family did not belong to a church or know a musician, we hired Bufford because we knew he would deliver. Mr. Wylie had known him since their days in high school together. He was a sharp man who always had a laugh for us. After the chapel services, he would come up to my office to get his check. Since he had the best seat in the house, he saw and heard everything, so there was always something entertaining that had happened that he couldn't wait to tell us. We lived for his stories.

During the wake hour, Bufford usually sang out a medley of funeral songs such as "When We All Get to Heaven," "I'll Fly Away," or "When I See Jesus," while some families would sit in silence, just letting Bufford speak for them. The last few minutes of the wake hour had to be handled delicately, since they were the saddest part of the service. Mr. Wylie stood before the room of grieving people and told them it would be their last opportunity to see their beloved again before the casket would be sealed for the remainder of the service. Mr. Wylie allowed the casket to remain open during the funeral only for special requests, since he had learned that it could be too overwhelming emotionally for loved ones. Keeping it closed ensured that no one would just walk up to the casket during the middle of the service, and also that we would arrive at the cemetery on time. Too often we ran behind schedule while we were trying to pry the hands of loved ones away, and sometimes we even had to prevent them from trying to get in the coffin.

Pastor Bates, our on-call minister, would go up for his eulogy. He usually arrived at the service a few minutes ahead of time to familiarize himself with the name of the deceased and read the obituary for details to work into his sermon. But to my ears it sounded like Pastor Bates preached the same sermon at every funeral. Whether the beloved was old or young, male or female, the members of the audience needed to get their lives together by accepting Christ as their Savior. We loved Pastor Bates at the funeral home because he wasn't a long-winded preacher. In about fifteen minutes his sermon was completed and we were ahead of schedule for the cemetery. Time was important, especially on Saturdays, when cemeteries charged families late fees for arriving after one P.M. There were some preachers who got carried away and ignored all time constraints. This was true within the apostolic or holiness church— you might as well bring your sleeping bag for those sermons. They celebrated a life by dancing and shouting up and down the aisle until the entire congregation was filled with the Holy Ghost. One person would catch it, then another, and another, and pretty soon several hours would have passed.

We'd wait at the top of the stairs for Pastor Bates to wrap up his time-efficient sermon. When he began his traditional Baptist preacher "whoop," we knew it was time to pack up. It sounded sort of like someone giving you the Heimlich maneuver: "I . . . *hah* . . . been . . . *hah* . . . through the valley . . . *hah* . . . of the shadows . . . *hah* . . . of death . . . *hah*."

This was the signal for Mr. Wylie to open the chapel doors

as we waited for Pastor Bates to give the benediction. Then Mr. Wylie would walk in and give the last words.

After the service finished, I'd often stand around pretending to be important while scoping for eye candy. The guests sometimes checked me out too. There were always men who managed to scribble their names on the back of a funeral program and slip it to me on the way out.

Sometimes I'd need to write work excuses for attendees after the service. "Can I get one of those slips to go back to work?" someone would ask, and then everyone else would flock around me with their hands held out. There was always someone who needed one for a spouse who wasn't there. People had the nerve to ask me to backdate the slip or even write several dates because they had taken off for a week or so. I found myself doing the same thing years later while in college: I made up my own excuse slips whenever I skipped class. By the time I graduated, I had killed my entire family.

As soon as we cleared the chapel, we'd close the doors and lower the body back down into the basement. We rolled the casket out the side door, and then the pallbearers lifted it into the hearse. Another day's work was done for us, but it was just the beginning of a long road ahead for the family.

For years, I was used as a buffer during the arrangements process. Mr. Wylie would send me into the room first to get a feel for the family, and I'd take in the basic information, complete the green card and other minor paperwork, then excuse myself, slip upstairs, and brief him on where I thought the family was financially. Then I would give him each family member's name and seating position so that when he entered the room it would feel to the family like he'd known them forever.

When Mr. Wylie made arrangements, he'd always find a way to make the entire room smile. I was amazed at how he could make grieving people laugh at jokes that weren't that funny. As he charmed them, he would take out a piece of scrap paper and start adding up our basic services. If he liked the family, he would knock an item off the list. It wouldn't be anything major—maybe the programs, maybe the organist or musician—but if he really liked them he might subtract a limo or hearse. With gas prices skyrocketing, though, that was happening less and less. But he knew that everyone loves to feel like they are getting a deal, and for a brief moment it was something he could do to distract each family from the pain of their loss and build some goodwill too.

I'd begun to take in more of the clients and started making funeral arrangements too. One day, I heard the loud buzz of the front doorbell while I was calculating the outstanding balances for the month. Even with our fancy intercom system, we still did not have an automated buzzer that would save us a trip downstairs. By the time I reached the bottom of the stairs, someone had already let a tall, handsome man in the building. He was dressed in sweats with a white T-shirt embroidered in red and blue.

His name was Kai, and he told me that his estranged mother had passed and his family expected him to arrange the burial. It was his first time making funeral arrangements and he said he needed some personal assistance. Although with all the work I had on my desk I really didn't have the time to provide him with such personal attention, he was pretty cute, so I figured it wouldn't be too taxing to help him out.

Mr. Wylie's sister-in-law had taken Kai in when he was an infant because his mother would leave him on the front porch—even as a baby—while she ran the streets. Somehow, he had forgiven her, and even though they weren't as close as a typical mother and son, he felt like he should handle her funeral arrangements, especially since no one else wanted the responsibility. As he sat across from me, I pulled out the all-important green card and a form for him to sign to authorize the release of his mother's body to us and give us legal permission to remove her remains. In some cases we'd already have the body in the basement, but I still needed a John Hancock. If a body was being held at the medical examiner's office, authorization was required before a removal. There were no exceptions.

Kai's mother had taken out a ten-thousand-dollar life insurance policy before she died, naming him as the beneficiary. When he handed over the policy, I searched for the date of issue, which would determine if it was contestable or not. So many people who came into the funeral home thinking they'd inherited insurance policies that would cover all the costs were oblivious to the fact that insurance policies have a contestability clause in their fine print. An insurance agent tells you that you are covered the moment you sign the paper, but what they don't say is that if you happen to die before the two-year anniversary of the policy issue date, then they will contest the payment you are due by requesting medical records and so forth. Also, if the policyholder lied about having cancer on the policy application, the insurance company would not have to honor the policy. Even if a policy is sound, in most cases an insurance company pays you only what you put into the policy. To protect himself, Mr. Wylie stopped accepting contestable policies altogether. He had been left too many times with outstanding balances when the insurance company did not pay the full cost.

I called the insurance company to verify the date Kai's mother's policy went into effect. Unfortunately, she had only become insured eighteen months before, so the policy was contestable. He would have to go to Plan B, which was paying out of his pocket.

I began my usual sales pitch.

"I understand that you will have to personally incur the funeral cost. I just need you to tell me where you would like to be financially—the high end, the low end, or somewhere in the middle." I motioned with my hands just like Mr. Wylie did. No one ever said the low end. Everyone always said the middle.

The middle was actually a good place, because even though it wasn't a Mercedes-Benz funeral package, it wasn't a Kia either. It was kind of like a solid, respectable Ford. The middle package deal included a low-grade metal casket in bronze or silver. It lacked the appeal of a fancy Batesville casket, but it looked okay and the cost couldn't be beat. Wylie charged three hundred dollars for the casket, while the least expensive Batesville was eleven hundred. For a little over four thousand dollars, one could afford a full funeral, including a limousine and a hearse; embalming, dressing, and casketing; professional services; the removal fee; and the church service fee, though an organist, a minister, the funeral programs, and the death certificates were extra.

Kai chose the minimum metal casket package. He wasn't

sure of how he would raise the money, but he said he wanted to have a decent burial for the woman who gave birth to him. In the middle of the arrangements, I got a call from Mr. Wylie telling me that he'd called to check on the body and according to the ME it was starting to decompose, so it did not make sense for Kai to have a service since her body was not viewable. After I explained this, Kai chose the option of doing a cremation with a memorial service.

In order to cremate his mother, Kai would have to identify her first. Unlike a traditional viewing, this process took all of five minutes. It would be the last time he'd see her. He also needed to sign paperwork with paragraphs of legal gibberish verifying that he was the appropriate next of kin and that a search for the closest relation had been made. Marital status was important when it came to cremations, since legally, a spouse has the first right to disposition. If I checked "married" on the death certificate, then the spouse was responsible for signing the paperwork, no matter what. I had dealt with several cases where someone was separated or in the process of a divorce and a mother or sibling was handling the funeral arrangements. But if the death certificate indicated that the person was married, their loved ones had to find the estranged spouse to either sign the paperwork or write a notarized letter relieving him or her from the responsibility.

I walked Kai out of the front door and to the side of the building, where we entered the basement. His mother was completely covered except for her head, and no embalming or other prep work had been done. Sometimes, if there was too much decomposition, Mr. Wylie had to quickly reshape features just for the sake of the loved one. Either way, the ID was always quick. No one could really bear the reality of seeing a loved one like that for the last time. After the identification, we'd put the body in a cremation container and it would go off to the crematory.

· · · ·

WHEN there was no memorial service, which often happened with cremations since they were the cheapest option, often the next of kin forgot about the cremains. In our back storage room, there were boxes of unclaimed ashes collecting dust.

For other people, the ashes held special meaning. One afternoon, Mr. Wylie asked me to ride with him, which was not unusual since I had often driven with Mr. Wylie on afternoons when he wanted some company.

I hopped into his Cadillac and we rolled through West Baltimore.

"Grab that bag under your seat," he told me.

I reached under my feet and picked up one of our small shopping bags with our logo on the front.

"Guess what's in there."

I looked inside the bag, which held a black square box.

"Cremains?"

"Hot dog. But whose cremains?"

"A dead person's . . ." I couldn't think of anyone specific at the time.

"Not quite."

He started laughing hysterically. Then he began to tell me the story of Ms. Jones, who'd called the funeral home several days before to ask if Mr. Wylie would handle the services for Rusty, her prized dog for more than fifteen years. In the bag beside me were the remains of Rusty. We reached her house and he asked me to grab the bag as we walked to the front door, where her husband greeted us.

"She's in there." He pointed us toward the living room, where we found Ms. Jones curled up on the sofa in her flannel pajamas, sobbing.

"Oh . . . is that my Rusty in there?" she cried. "That was my baby. I can't believe she's gone. Why . . . oh lawd why."

Mr. Wylie responded with his usual "yes, ma'am" and handed her Rusty.

"Can you say a prayer for him?" she asked. At this point I was getting nervous that I would lose it. Mr. Wylie and her husband helped Ms. Jones up from the sofa and we all grabbed hands. Mr. Wylie began the prayer, "Lord, everything you made was good," while I squeezed his hand tight to keep myself from laughing. "Therefore Rusty was good. Thank you for your good works. Amen."

CHAPTER
NINE

"WHO'S got the body?" Those words fell from the lips of funeral goers like curse words from sailors. It was the second most asked question after, "How'd they die?" The choice of funeral home was a status symbol in our town.

Undertakers have historically been the premier entrepreneurs in the black community. They were one of the exclusion businesses that could thrive, along with barbershops and beauty salons. The reason is that the community needed their services desperately. In the nineteenth and early twentieth centuries, white funeral homes had treated their black clients with little respect. Black families were often forced to use back doors and basement entries, or to meet with white undertakers after hours to make funeral arrangements for their loved ones. Black corpses were treated badly too. These memories of the mistreatment of bodies by white funeral directors were passed on through generations of blacks. Because of this, black families chose to use black funeral directors to bury their loved ones once they could, and so the funeral business became as segregated as the churches; blacks started burying blacks. Families trusted their loved ones with people who looked like them and would treat them with decency.

Whites also had no real desire to memorialize or participate in a service commemorating the black dead. After prepping the body, they often returned it to the family or church of the deceased and allowed them to arrange the final disposition. This meant that either the family or the church was responsible for the service and burial. In the South, many families would have a wake right in their living room and have the body on display for the family and friends to see.

At Wylie's, we worked almost exclusively with black families. The whites we buried were usually part of the city's Commission on Aging program. Most of them did not have family or could not take care of themselves, so they were wards of the state.

The connection between funeral homes and churches dates back many years. Black preachers have always played a significant role in the burial process. Not only did they recommend the undertaker and help arrange the services, but they also preached many of the services. That's why so many preachers became funeral directors, and almost all funeral directors are members of a church.

Baltimore was not short on black-owned funeral homes. They lined our streets like bus stops and seemed to be dispersed into every major corridor of the city. If you rode three blocks north of Wylie Funeral Home and turned left, you'd run smack into one. Up four blocks, to the right, you'd pass another. At least four were spread out across North Avenue alone. I knew firms that had the same last name, but no blood relation, while others had a blood relation but no business ties.

There was plenty of work to feed the mouths of all the hungry funeral directors. Even if a smaller firm received only one or two calls a week, it still managed to survive. Whether it meant cutting overhead and single-handedly executing every task, marking up prices, trade embalming for another director, renting out funeral cars, or even making custom-engraved nameplates, they always found a way to stay afloat. But Wylie Funeral Home was masterfully killing all its rivals by wooing customers with fancy reconstructive handiwork and top-of-the-line products.

The competition among the men in the industry was stiffer than anything I'd ever seen. The same man you laughed with today might call the State Board of Morticians on you the following morning to report you for possible violations. They'd speak in hushed tones: "I think such and such has an unlicensed worker embalming." Or "They've got unapproved signage in front of their building." The State Board of Morticians had very strict guidelines, and sometimes they sent out inspectors to make sure the funeral home was up to par. Mr. Wylie talked so loudly that I always overheard his end of the conversation when he was gossiping with other directors. But it really wasn't necessary for me to eavesdrop because he always told me any juicy news afterward.

It was a tight-knit world, and word traveled fast. When a director decided that a worker wasn't fit for the business, the directors collectively blackballed the worker from the industry.

If a director fired a young apprentice or driver, he would call around to all his friends to warn them before the person went looking for new work and dropping off résumés.

Many morticians had some type of substance abuse problem. Some were heavy drinkers; others smoked a pack a day. There were rumors that a few did hard drugs. And God only knows what they did with the embalming fluid they kept in the basement. Who could blame them? They had to look at dead bodies every day, and the pressure of trying to restore a corpse to a particular family's standards was cause for a drink or two.

Some directors had split personalities. When they dealt with grieving families, they were the gentlest men that you could ever meet, but when they dealt with workers in the industry, they changed completely. Mr. Wylie had his moments too. When someone got out of line, showed up late, ignored a command, or did anything other than what he had instructed them to do, he reminded them firmly that his name was on the outside of the building. "Shucks, I'm Al Wylie," he'd say, handing them one of his business cards.

Mr. Wylie sometimes hired other morticians to embalm for him when he was too busy to do it himself. I couldn't get along with any of the men he hired. For one thing, most men in the business did not respect women, and these men could not understand why Mr. Wylie trusted me to hold down the fort by myself.

One time he hired Mike Zigler, an older man who acted like a rebellious child every time I gave him a specific instruction. I'd often deliver messages to him directly from Mr. Wylie.

"Mr. Wylie said don't forget to set the face first," I told him as soon as I hung up a call with Mr. Wylie.

"I'm a licensed mortician. Tell Al Wylie I know what I'm

doing. I don't think he would have called me over if I didn't," he said with an attitude. I just kept thinking, *What kind of a man sasses a seventeen-year-old?* I told Mr. Wylie about it and he put Zigler in his place when he returned.

Then there was Vaughn Green, an up-and-coming funeral director who used our basement for embalming while he was trying to start his own business. Vaughn didn't have that flip personality. That's because he was quietly watching and plotting to take over the entire industry. It seemed like he became a sensation overnight. We went to sleep one evening and woke up to his billboards, a mall kiosk, and multiple locations in East and West Baltimore.

Over in East Baltimore was another father-son establishment, Calvin B. Scruggs Funeral Home. Calvin Jr. represented the next generation of funeral directors. He directed funerals by morning and coached basketball at my high school in the afternoon. He wore Versace shirts and linen suits at his services and drove a blue BMW with a customized license plate. When his father passed away from cancer, Calvin Jr. hadn't finished the mortuary program at Catonsville yet, so he wasn't able to run the business right away. However, the state of Maryland issued his mother a widow's license, which allows a spouse to continue running the business after the death of a director. She ran the business until Calvin Jr. passed the National Board exam.

The funeral directors who weren't obnoxious were just weird. They had processed hair, suits from the seventies, and gold teeth. Mr. Wylie considered some funeral directors competition, but others didn't even make the cut.

Mr. Wylie's biggest competitor was a man he called "the boss." The boss's name was William Brown, and he was the man who had given Mr. Wylie his second chance at life. Mr. Wylie was thirty-nine years old when he decided to go to mortuary school, and William Brown taught him everything about the business. They were frenemies who were proud of each other's accomplishments and shared all the industry secrets but would sometimes go months without speaking to each other because of some stupid squabble that bruised their egos or pride.

When I was growing up, Leroy O. Dyett and Son Funeral Home was the name that rung out the most for me. He was the go-to director for our church congregation then, for which he had Mr. Wylie to thank. After Mr. Wylie stopped working for "the boss," he became Mr. Dyett's lead mortician and brought the church's business to him. When I was very young, I thought Mr. Wylie was Mr. Dyett because he usually stood up on his behalf when a funeral service was announced in church.

Before stepping out on his own, Mr. Dyett had partnered with another mortician to form Morton and Dyett Funeral Home. They had a long run as the most popular funeral service in Baltimore in the sixties and early seventies before they went their separate ways and opened their own businesses. Mr. Dyett would eventually give the world Al Wylie, and Mr. Morton gave the world Vaughn Green.

The division of the Morton and Dyett Funeral Home left a wide gap for a man named William March to step in and grow his business to become the premier funeral home in the city. March was a postal worker who wanted to make a difference in the African American community, and so in the late fifties, he started a funeral home in his East Baltimore row home. By 1978, he had built a facility that occupied an entire city block. A few years later, he did it again, opening another location on the other side of town. Today, his children continue his legacy, running one of the largest black-owned funeral chains in the United States.

Whenever I passed the east location, the parking lot would be full. The champagne pink fleet of cars was unmistakable. March Funeral Home was the first to step outside the box when it came to traditional funeral home marketing. They used photos of their handsome family on billboards and got on the radio to become a household name. I remember using their stick fans to cool down in church on Sundays. On the front of the fan was a black family, with a random mother, father, son, and daughter dressed in casual clothing. They looked like they had just taken a picture at the church picnic. The family was not grieving or sad—they were smiling, as if to say, *If you choose March Funeral Home, you too can be this happy.* It's hard to trace exactly how fans became such a popular advertising tool for the death business. They were just so ubiquitous. But I remember picking that fan up each Sunday. It was much better than the one with the pale Jesus.

When Mr. Wylie started using fans to advertise, he had just his logo on the front. But then he added a photo with his staff all standing behind him as he sat in a backward-facing chair flashing his blinged-out ID bracelet, which read "Al Wylie" in diamonds. After he remarried, he replaced the picture of his staff with one of his new family. I always felt disappointed that I never made the funeral fan.

From what I could tell, the stick fans and yearly calendars weren't as big an influence when it came to advertising as word of mouth. When a loved one dies, you're not likely to remember the name of the funeral home on the back of the fan you used to cool off with or on the sign over the Franklin Street bridge as quickly as you remember the name of the man who buried Cousin Trudy, because "she looked good."

If a director didn't have his neighborhood on lock, then he was doing something wrong. And if he wasn't a member of a fraternity or neighborhood group or on some kind of board, then he probably didn't do much business either. Families want to know the person who cares for their family members. In our community, you couldn't always choose your doctors or nurses, but you could choose your mortician. There's nothing like entrusting your loved one to a friend, or at least someone who could pretend to be your friend. It took me years to realize that ninety percent of the people who said they knew Mr. Wylie personally did not really have a relationship with him at all.

In recent years, big corporations like Service Corporation International have tried to get into the business of black funeral service. They've wanted to buy out firms, sometimes keeping the business intact with its original name. Mr. Wylie never considered selling out. He was adamant about building a legacy for his own son.

• • • •

MR. Wylie was always telling me about his dreams for expanding his business. He'd talked about it for as long as I can remember. Once, while we were sitting at the kitchen table eating breakfast, he told me how he planned to buy the two vacant houses next door and knock the walls out between them to make a chapel large enough to seat two hundred people. He wanted to be sure that large families who couldn't afford the additional fee to use the church down the street could fit comfortably. Moreover, expanding the building would launch him into a new market altogether. During our talks in the embalming room while Brandon was still at school, he told me how he and Brandon would soon work together so that he could direct one funeral while Brandon would be out supervising another.

A short time later, he called me into the office and told me to pull up a chair. Instead of handing me a stack of invoices to file, he pulled out a long roll of paper.

"What's this?" I eagerly asked.

"Our new funeral home," he said while unrolling the huge plans from his architect. My eyes could hardly take in all the different rooms pictured, and I got up to get a better view. Mr. Wylie was excited to give me a guided tour, and so he pulled one of his Albert P. Wylie Funeral Home pens from his lapel and gave me a walk-through of the designs.

"This right here is the chapel." Mr. Wylie pointed to the huge space on the diagram. "And if someone's handicapped, they come right up this ramp and, hot dog it, they are in the chapel." He smiled and looked thrilled to be able to offer this new feature.

"Come here." He pulled me closer and wrapped his arm around my shoulder. "This is your office." My eyes lit up with excitement, even though I knew it was only my office during the evening. By day, it would be Ms. Angela's. "I'm getting y'all new computers, new everything."

Mr. Wylie had an ambitious vision. He planned to put in

two new arrangement rooms with real doors that provided the privacy he thought his paying customers deserved. The biggest upgrade for his clients was the "Meaningful Memories" Casket Selection Room that Batesville Casket Company would provide. In the casket selection room, families would be able to come in and choose their casket right off the showroom floor. Full-size caskets would line the walls, as would other products we offered, including urns, markers, vaults, and even clothing. He knew this would be very attractive to his clients, especially since there was still an old myth within the black community that shady undertakers recycled caskets. Batesville also did casket engraving. In the chapel, he would swap the peach carpet for a dark plum to camouflage the dirt from the heavy foot traffic. In addition to the fancy carpet, he wanted to add a giant mirror engraved with the company logo and mount it to the chapel wall, right above the fireplace. The renovations also called for new offices for himself and Brandon. His old office would become the staff conference room, and he'd build a new prep room from the floor up. All the construction would begin in just a few weeks.

Mr. Wylie kept how much volume he was doing a secret, but the streets were watching. An expansion like this would signal that he was doing well for himself. However, all he cared about was doing well for his son.

The expansion wasn't the only major change that would be taking place in the upcoming months. Two years had flown by, and Brandon was finishing his final semester at school. Mr. Wylie couldn't mask his excitement for his baby boy's return; it led every conversation for months. If he graduated, he'd be the youngest licensed mortician in the state. Mr. Wylie dreamed of the day that Brandon's name would stand beside his on a marquee. It would read, "Albert P. Wylie and Brandon," he used to joke, because his "son had a name"—and it was Brandon. But instead he decided to change the name of the business to Wylie Funeral Home, and drop "Albert P." to give Brandon just as much ownership. He also changed the company tagline to "Our Family Serving Your Family." Every move he made was strategically played to position his son.

Most directors wanted to leave their businesses to their sons. But for Mr. Wylie, building a legacy to leave Brandon was also his way of making up for the fact that he had missed out on some of Brandon's crucial years growing up. Mr. Wylie was proud that Brandon hadn't gotten caught up in the streets. As an incentive to do well in school, Mr. Wylie promised Brandon that once he graduated and became licensed he could have any car he wanted, as long as it was black, so he could lead the funeral processions. So nineteen-year-old Brandon would just have to decide if he wanted to drive a Lexus, a BMW, or a Mercedes.

But it was no secret that Brandon had struggled academically in high school, and that didn't change during college.

"I just don't get it," he'd always say to Mr. Wylie on their daily phone call.

"Did you open the book?" his father would ask him.

"No."

"You gotta read the book. Open the book."

Even with the generous car pledge, Mr. Wylie had doubts about Brandon making it through the mortuary program, especially since one of his colleague's daughters had gone off to mortuary school in Atlanta and flunked every semester. Her father had no idea that his baby girl wouldn't be graduating with the rest of her class, and in his enthusiasm, he sent invitations to family members, friends, and colleagues announcing her matriculation. He even ordered a coach bus for everyone to travel from Baltimore to Atlanta to the graduation. It wasn't until the week of the graduation that the daughter finally found the nerve to tell her dad the truth. Though he was disappointed, her dad still bought her a new car and she moved back home to help run the business. Brandon never would have gotten away with something like that.

Thinking about Brandon's return left me unsettled. In many ways, his homecoming posed a threat: The boy I had crushed on since fifth grade would now be my biggest competitor. While I couldn't wait to see if he had finally grown into his ears, I was destroyed by the idea that my role at Wylie Funeral Home might change. I worried that the status I'd worked so hard for would be overshadowed by something that I didn't have: the same bloodline or the Wylie name. I secretly hoped that Brandon would pull a charade like Mr. Wylie's colleague's daughter, and that he'd flunk.

But that May, Mr. Wylie chartered a bus with a big sign on the side that said "Brandon Wylie Come on Back Home" to take all of Brandon's family and friends down to Fayetteville to see him walk across the stage. I didn't attend because it fell on my Saturday shift—and I never missed a Saturday.

I was readying for my senior year of high school the summer we prepared for the grand opening of the newly renovated building. The new, improved Wylie Funeral Home became a place where mourners felt more at home. It had a comforting energy that felt more like a living room than a viewing room. I dubbed the new conference room the Old Country Buffet room because the furniture looked old and country and it seemed like there should be food spread out on the table. But it was welcoming and homey. It became the heart of the funeral home and also Mr. Wylie's personal dressing room—you could find him there many afternoons looking at swatches for his personalized "APW" embroidered shirts. Just as he'd promised, the office that I shared with Ms. Angela was furnished with new desks and carpets and brand-new computers.

Brandon was back from school and Mr. Wylie quickly gave him the authority to run things as the second in charge. However, he didn't teach him how to embalm. He had Hari P. Close, another funeral director, teach him the basics. "Let him show you all the wrong things to do and I'll come back and show you how to do it the right way," Mr. Wylie told him.

Brandon moved into the funeral home, and so he was working around the clock some days, often taking death calls and making removals on his own at night. But he started getting the perks of the job too. He got used to having his own fancy embroidered shirts and his standing barbershop appointment on Fridays. Mr. Wylie coddled and spoiled him. One night he crashed his Mercedes after falling asleep at the wheel. The car was totaled, but days later he had a brand-new car. Three more times he destroyed his car, and each and every time a new one was waiting. He stayed out all night with his friends on Friday nights, but if there was a service that Saturday, he needed to be back home by eight A.M. sharp.

And he was getting a real crash course in urban funeral directing. Once when there were two services scheduled for the same time, Mr. Wylie asked him to handle the funeral of a young homicide victim at Harlem Park Community Baptist

Church. As always, he walked the family into the sanctuary of the church and seated them for the wake hour. Thinking they were all settled and he had the service under control, he sent the hearse driver out to run an errand for him at the bank. But once one of the family members of the deceased began giving remarks, a threatening-looking gang of young men and women wearing bandanas and T-shirts began walking back and forth to the casket, shaking it. The woman at the podium started getting frustrated and addressed the youngsters from the microphone. "Why don't you stop disrespecting my family and sit the fuck down!" In response, the mob bum-rushed her, and fighting broke out up and down the aisles of the church.

After a few minutes of intense brawling, people began to move outside and fight in the middle of the street. Brandon stood in the pulpit, stunned, just watching the mayhem. When it calmed a little, he went to the church sexton and told him to lock the door. He locked himself and the rest of the people who seemed to be calm inside the building while he waited for the police. The family was still seated in the front row, and Brandon directed Pastor Bates to start the sermon to keep everyone distracted.

The only problem Brandon had was the hearse driver, who was still out running errands, which meant that Brandon was stuck there in the church with the body. Even though the scene was total chaos, he had to protect the body. Finally, police and ambulances arrived outside and Brandon kept the family barricaded inside until he saw the hearse pull up. The police then escorted the procession to the cemetery.

Some of the older drivers who worked with us were not enthused about having a nineteen-year-old Wylie calling the shots. "I'm not listening to you. You ain't even half my age," one driver told him. Even some preachers felt threatened by his authority. He was once directing a service and a preacher told him, "Sit down. You don't get up in my pulpit and make announcements." That only made him work harder to earn the respect that he rightfully deserved.

But to me, Brandon acted like the same old boss's son he always had, which was a relief. And I wasn't all that impressed by what he'd learned in school. One Saturday I drove the hearse for a service he was directing. When we arrived at the cemetery, he gave his usual speech. "We at the Wylie Funeral Home hope that the services we have rendered to you have been of some constellation to you in this your hour of loss." Of course, he meant to say "consolation," but he kept saying "constellation." I couldn't wait to get back to the funeral home and make him aware of his error.

Brandon and I didn't cross paths much since Mr. Wylie usually gave him the weekend off when we didn't have a Saturday service. When we were working together, we fell into a sort of sibling rivalry, and just like a sister, every now and then I would throw a punch at him for no particular reason. That punch would lead us into a headlock and before I knew it we would be wrestling in the Old Country Buffet room like five-year-olds. Ms. Angela would fuss at us. "Why don't y'all just do it and get it over with? In fact, you should let me watch."

"Ewww," I always responded.

"Why watch porn when you can watch friends?" is what she liked to say. Ms. Angela was always direct.

One afternoon I showed up to work in a lavender double-breasted pantsuit with black mesh sandals. I had worn it before and managed to slip under the radar. I had already been at work for an hour when Mr. Wylie noticed my outfit.

"I don't like it."

"Okay." I laughed it off.

"No! You need to go and change your clothes."

"Are you serious?"

His stern look implied that he certainly was. He instructed Brandon to answer the door and the phone while I was gone. That evening, a deacon from a neighboring church was going to be on view, and he apparently didn't think my outfit was holy enough for his church members.

I grabbed my stuff and stormed out the front door. He was sending me home to the other side of town, a half hour away, to change my clothes in the middle of rush hour? I arrived back at the funeral home in one of my usual black dresses, and for the rest of the evening I stood by the front door, waiting for someone to come see me in the outfit Mr. Wylie had forced me to wear. But no one showed up to see the deacon for the rest of the night. I just kept thinking that this never would have happened if Brandon hadn't come back. I was beginning to be put in my place.

After a year of being home, Brandon decided he wanted to take classes at Morgan State and get a degree in business. Nothing could have pleased Mr. Wylie more. He was happy to change Brandon's schedule so that he'd have plenty of time for school and studying.

It was now Mr. Wylie's turn to be proud of me. With college acceptances from Drexel, the University of Florida, and Catholic University, I could have exchanged my morbid wardrobe for sweatshirts, shorts, and flip-flops in some other town.

Mr. Wylie called me into his office to ask me about my college plans. He knew I had lots of interests, and even though it had always felt like I was cheating on him somehow, I had worked other part-time jobs—internships in law, business, and social services—every summer that I worked there except the first one. None of them had given me the feeling that funeral service did. I didn't get chills when I walked through the front door, and I never stayed late or just stopped by on a whim. They were just jobs. The funeral home was something much more.

I sat across from him, waved the smoke from his cigarette out of my face, and somehow heard myself telling him that I would work an additional day since the other evening person was leaving. Every time I had a way out, I went in deeper.

I decided to stay at home and attend an all-girls college. I'd thought I'd become a lawyer so I could learn to put away the murderers for good and stop the crime. But I figured becoming a mortician could always be Plan B—I would just transfer to Catonsville.

But there was something else in the back of my mind—the fear of a dreaded phone call from Mr. Wylie telling me he had my own mother's body. We still ignored her condition most of the time. Then one evening, it was just the two of us at home, and I was lying in bed with her like I usually did when my father was at work. We were both flipping through magazines when I brought up college.

"I think I'm deciding between Drexel and University of Florida," I said. They were the two out-of-state colleges where I had been accepted.

"Drexel's not too far away. You may get to Florida and never come back."

"You never know." I laughed.

"If I get sick while you're away, will you come home and take care of me?"

"Of course I will, Mommy," I reassured her. I knew she was asking hypothetically because she was too proud a woman to ask something like that, but for whatever reason she needed reassurance that night. It was at that moment I knew I couldn't go away to college because one day my mother would need me to take care of her. And even though I knew she would never ask me to hold myself back for her, my promise was unbreakable.

Mr. Wylie didn't make it any easier. He always found ways to keep me interested and loyal. When I officially declared my major, Mr. Wylie called me into his office. He handed me a stack of legal documents from his lawyer. "Read these and tell me what they mean," he told me as I flipped through the stack.

"Now?"

"Yes, right now." He dismissed me to go read.

Mr. Wylie didn't want to limit my scope to funeral service. He wanted to help me practice for the bar exam. I was already coding his checks for his accountant, a special assignment that gave me insight into where he spent every dollar. He even let me sign his name on checks.

CHAPTER
TEN

"I work for the Coca-Cola soda company," the stocky brown fella informed me on our first date.

"And I work at a funeral home."

"Which one?"

"Wylie."

"What do you do?"

"If I tell you I'll have to kill you." We both chuckled.

"You're too cute for all of that."

"All of that" meant working with dead bodies.

He sat across the table from me at Mo's Seafood Restaurant, a popular venue for the local movers and shakers. Lexus coupes, Beamers, and Benzes adorned the front of the place on any given night. The big bosses brought their ladies there to treat them to crab cakes, lobster, and other expensive seafood dishes. Others used it as a meeting place for their homeboys to discuss business or entertain one another. The ballers knew the waitresses and bartenders by name and tipped them well. It was the black version of mafia headquarters, which would explain why it had also been a fatal crime scene.

As soon as I'd transferred the phones to the answering service and locked up the funeral home that night, I met him at the downtown location. I was still dressed in my black skirt and blouse from the viewing earlier that day, and I was dying to slip out of my itchy stockings. So I removed them in the car, something my mother certainly would have disapproved of. In her mind, no stockings meant easy access, but I wore stockings to work only because Mr. Wylie insisted, and I would do anything to keep him from hollering.

My date seemed more intrigued than creeped out when I shared my place of work with him. I liked to disclose this information up front because it had the potential to be a deal breaker: "I don't date smokers, women with children, or girls who work at funeral homes." If that was the case, it was certainly understandable. I mean, the scent of embalming fluid melted into my skin like perfume. Mr. Wylie's cigarette smoke often got trapped between the strands of my hair. In my closet were an unreasonable number of black garments for someone who was not depressed or in mourning. Then there was the self-imposed curfew that didn't allow me to stay out late on Friday nights because I needed to be bright eyed for my Saturday morning shift. Whomever I dated needed to understand all of that.

I knew very little about Ahmad. His cousin was a schoolmate of mine who wanted to hook me up with him. I was skeptical about a blind date, but I was willing to try anything once. I should have recognized it sooner, but even after all my years at the funeral home I was still green about a lot of things. How could he have possibly afforded his Lincoln Navigator on his soda company salary? He also had every color sweater made by Coogi, a brand that the rapper Notorious B.I.G. made popular in urban communities through his lyric "However, I stay Coogi down to the socks." Ahmad also wore an expensive chain around his neck sometimes. When he told me he worked for the soda company, I believed him. It wasn't until later that I realized Coca-Cola was a euphemism for the coke he really sold.

I had never even seen a real drug dealer before I began working at the funeral home. Ironically, the fact that my father was a police officer kept me even more shielded because he was absolutely determined to keep the side of the city he knew all too well from his children. The television show *New York Undercover* had been my only exposure. But in my years with Al Wylie I'd seen my fair share, and I'd seen firsthand the ruthless violence that followed them. We once had a case of a young kingpin who had been kidnapped and held for ransom. The culprits called and demanded twenty thousand dollars in cash from the boy's father. The father went into the boy's stash and met the kidnappers at the asking point, and still they killed the boy in cold blood. If we were burying a drug dealer and suspected that trouble could start, then we asked the police for backup to keep things in order. In most cases, the families we served kept it real with us and gave us a heads-up that their son was a criminal, so we could prepare ourselves.

Mr. Wylie would say, "Call Ricky's boys," making it sound like my father ran things in the department. It was rare that my father himself would get involved, but every now and then we would work on the same cases. We once handled the services of a high-profile young criminal who was murdered, and we assumed that the many thugs he was connected to would attend the funeral to pay their final respects. My father and some of his colleagues came to the funeral not just for protection, but because he was following several suspects with outstanding warrants who were associated with the dead man. But my father was always evasive, never telling me exactly what he was investigating when he came to the services.

We weren't always so lucky to get a whiff of danger ahead of time. There was one time when Mr. Wylie was out of town and we had a young man on view. The foot traffic was as heavy as ever, and as Ms. Angela and I were about to exchange shifts, we heard a commotion break loose. Sets of fists started banging on the front door, and what sounded like a stampede of feet raced around downstairs. Then the door opened and we heard the screams.

"They shooting! They shooting!"

Bap! Bap! Bap! More shots exploded, and we took cover.

"Oh, hell no." Ms. Angela dodged in front of the door and shut it as people tried to run upstairs into our office. We crawled behind her desk and she phoned the police, while more people tried to barge through the office door.

Apparently, the brother of the homicide victim on view was next on the shooter's list. The funeral home was now a crime scene. Thank God, no one was hurt. The shooting squad had to examine the street outside to look for shell casings and the local news stations sent reporters to cover the story.

• • • •

DRUGS still fueled devastating violence in our city. David Simon's HBO series *The Wire* was dead-on in its depiction of Baltimore at the time, so much so that years later, my father refused to watch the show. The storylines were based on actual cases that loomed large in his mind, and he didn't want to live through them twice.

While the homicide rate had dropped significantly in 2000, from 305 to 261, murder victims still continued to fill our clipboard. We were still the number one city in the country in terms of crime statistics, a dubious honor we'd held for several years running. I'd drive past makeshift memorials on our neighborhood's corners, with flattened helium balloons and handcrafted posters with photos and stenciled letters. I watched the desperate pleas for justice from victims' loved ones on the news. Candlelight vigils and Stop the Violence rallies were far too familiar. But the drug culture went too deep in the community to be rooted out easily. Well-known criminals in Baltimore launched the now infamous Stop Snitchin' campaign with a viral video meant to intimidate witnesses from working with police. Even the professional basketball player Carmelo Anthony appeared in the video, which drew fire from the media but didn't do much to loosen the noose of fear around the necks of the residents of West Baltimore.

Gang culture was even changing the nature of the services themselves. The days when dress suits were universal burial attire were passing, for one thing. More and more young men who came through our doors were being buried in casual street or athletic clothes. That is not to say that it wasn't the latest, finest urban wear that money could buy. It wasn't strange to see a young man wearing a Polo shirt, a Phat Farm sweater, and jeans or khaki pants for his funeral. I heard one mother say, "My son never wore a suit while he was living, so why should he wear one now?"

Sometimes, the family wanted their boy buried in a baseball cap, and sometimes the damage to the deceased's head was so bad we requested one. Repairing gunshot wounds—especially ones that affected the face or head—required precision. Mr. Wylie would have to fill bullet holes with wax and then layer makeup on to cover it. Sometimes, he had to hang a veil over the casket so that family and friends couldn't tamper with his work. Families had on occasion touched the body, smearing the makeup he used to camouflage flesh wounds. On other occasions families added accessories to the body, restyled hair, or changed lip color.

The guests at the funeral services started dressing less formally too. I'm not sure where the idea came from, but some up-and-coming designer invented the memorial T-shirt, made with a loved one's photo printed on the front. It was a fashion phenomenon in funeral culture. The shirts normally included the date of death and the deceased's nickname. When I began working, I noticed just a few of the T-shirts at viewings, but they were soon being worn more frequently, even at the funerals. In some cases, people even made a "viewing" T-shirt and then made a "funeral" T-shirt with another photo. And the trend wasn't just limited to men—there were also young ladies wearing the T-shirts instead of dresses. My biggest shock came the day I saw a grandma in the front row of a funeral dressed in one of them.

God forbid the deceased was in a gang. Fellow gang members always showed up with their gang decorations. As soon as we left the room, they would tie bandanas around the deceased's wrists and wrap them around his head. We would wait until they left, but we always removed anything that the family hadn't specifically requested be dressed on the body.

One afternoon, we had a busy viewing for a homicide victim. After the foot traffic died down, I stepped into the room to check on the body. Sometimes people kissed the body, inadvertently messing up the makeup, and so we would periodically do a little fix or two to keep it looking perfect.

This time, when I walked in the room I noticed something in the casket. I walked closer to make sure that my eyes weren't fooling me. It wasn't unusual for someone to leave an artifact or something of sentimental value, but instead I saw a bottle of Hennessy cognac lying in the boy's arm and a bag of marijuana in his hand. This was taking it too far. I had heard of people lacing marijuana with embalming fluid, but I'd never heard of lacing a body with marijuana.

I called Mr. Wylie in the room and we shared a laugh before he tucked the items under the boy's pillow. He didn't want the family to see those things and he couldn't possibly take the body in church the next morning with them visible. Neither of us smoked marijuana or drank, so there was no need to keep them for us.

. . . .

THE longer I dated Ahmad, the more I worried that one day his name would be in the first column of the clipboard. His main headquarters wasn't far from the funeral home. In fact, many of his clients were regulars at our services. He supervised the neighborhoods a few blocks over. If he'd been a real businessman, he would have asked Mr. Wylie for a commission on the business he sent our way with his customers, who were slowly killing themselves with intravenous drug use and overdoses, and the hustlers who were slain over jealousy or money. He indirectly sent us a lot of work.

I would panic if I didn't hear from him for a few days. I couldn't help but think that the cops would find him in some abandoned parking lot, stuffed into his trunk, his life taken over a petty altercation about money or dope and his body filled with holes. Sometimes when I looked at him, I could see his face bloated in a casket. I'd watch him sleep, with his neck hidden beneath his chin, and picture those corpse faces that I saw every day. He slept with a gun under his pillow, and whenever he heard a car drive by, he'd jump up and peek through the venetian blinds to make sure it wasn't someone coming for him. He knew he was playing Russian roulette, and I knew it too. I was just infatuated.

He was strong and dangerous, but every day, I saw dangerously strong men stretched out after being slaughtered in the streets. The saying "You'll end up dead or in jail" was more than just a saying; it was reality. And no matter how many funerals the men of Baltimore attended, they lived each day like it was their last, patiently waiting their turn.

That year, Mr. Wylie had a Christmas party and I brought Ahmad as my date. I had been dating him for nine months and I knew I wouldn't be able to let him meet my parents, so I was hoping for Mr. Wylie's approval.

I briefly introduced him to Mr. Wylie, who was busy greeting a roomful of people. They chatted for a few moments, but I really couldn't sense whether Mr. Wylie liked him or not.

When we got back to work, Mr. Wylie asked, "How is Pound Cake?"

"How was the pound cake from the party?" I asked him.

"No, your date, Pound Cake. Did y'all see Pound Cake at the party? He kept sending Sheri to the bar to get him liquor," he joked.

"Yeah, we saw Pound Cake." Brandon laughed along with his father.

I was fuming on the inside. From then on, Pound Cake was a big joke around the funeral home.

• • • •

AHMAD called one afternoon. He said he was outside my house and he needed me to drive him somewhere. He never showed up at my house unannounced, but I didn't ask any questions. I thought that he had something special planned for us.

The clouds were darkening and it looked like the sky would open at any moment when he hopped in my truck and gave me directions to our destination. We soon arrived at an apartment complex that was five minutes away from my home. After kissing my forehead, he told me he'd be right back and got out. I assumed that this was just a preliminary stop before our big date and I remember worrying that I wasn't dressed to go anywhere nice. The rain began to fall as I sat there waiting for him. Then I caught sight of a young mother and her child walking out of the building. I watched as they went into the covered staircase and hid. I thought it was strange but I didn't dwell on it. Another fifteen minutes passed before Ahmad returned to the car.

As I pulled off I could see the mother and her son leaving the staircase in my rearview window.

"I could have killed that boy."

I thought he was speaking figuratively.

"He owed me twenty Gs. He's lucky he had his kid and wife there."

Now he was starting to scare me and it was all starting to make sense.

"I need you to hold something for me."

He showed me a gun. I had no idea where it came from or that he'd had it on him when he got into my car. He started wrapping the silver pistol in some kind of cloth. I couldn't believe what was happening, and I could hardly see the road with the rain coming down so hard. I slammed on my brakes at the red light, my heart racing.

There was no way I could stash a gun for him, but I was too afraid to tell him no. I definitely couldn't take it into my father's house, and I didn't want to get caught with it in my car. But I took the gun and put it under my seat anyway to appease him. I rushed to get to my house because I wanted him out of my car. Although he didn't actually pull the trigger, he had come close enough, and if the gun had gone off, my future would have been ruined. I would have been an accessory because, technically, I was driving the getaway car. I would have broken my father's heart. It was then I knew I needed Ahmad out of my life. And I went back to being that girl from the other side of town.

CHAPTER
ELEVEN

AFTER Aunt Mary died, I'd started writing poetry. The themes of death reincarnated themselves in different ways, over and over again, in my writing. I scribbled many of my poems while sitting behind my desk at the funeral home. There, in complete solitude, I found a place where I could reflect, daydream, and process all that was swirling around me. I wrote a poem called "Endangered Black Man" as a plea to young men to stop becoming fatalities.

Confined to the streets
Oppressed you will never be free
From your own bondage
Incarcerated not only by physical means
But Black man, you are mentally bound to your cage

And you're still not enraged
You just don't get it
Endangered Black man
You have destroyed me the voice of the Black tomorrow
And now all our people see is sorrow
And no cries of empathy do we ever hear
Never have they shed a tear
But because of you I live in fear
Endangered Black man

On another afternoon, a pile of death certificates I was looking through inspired me to compose this in my notebook:

I breathed today
I breathed
A breath of refreshment
A breath of realization
A breath of thanksgiving
I realized that
Breathing is much more refreshing,
Definitely a blessing
And I am grateful for my breath
Because someone stopped breathing today
So I breathe a breath of sincere satisfaction and relief
That they will rest in peace
Someone else is breathing
Artificial, inauthentic, unnatural breaths
And it's killing them softly
Someone's breathing is controlled

By machines of forced life support
And their life is cut short
Because they thought a man-made machine could save them

And I breathe, and I breathe, and I breathe

Because I thought I would never breathe again
And so I breathe for every sister
That stopped at the hands of some trifling man
I breathe for every child that never breathed
Because a selfish mother sacrificed her seed
I breathe for every punctured lung
Injured at the hands of envious ungodly spirits
I pray for every lung that collapsed
From carrying burdens from one lung to the next

I breathe for every asthmatic lung that had the wind knocked out it
I breathe for every short-lived conversation
I breathe for every long-winded preacher
I breathe for everyone that's waiting to exhale
I inhale
And I breathe, and I breathe, and I breathe

Over the years I was working at the funeral home, I wrote hundreds of poems, and so I decided to publish my first book of poetry and short stories while I was a junior in college. Once again, I stuck close to the theme of death. In a short story featured in the back of the book, I wrote about a young girl who contracted HIV but found a man who loved her through the circumstances. I knew it wasn't the most inviting subject to read or write about, but I wanted to make it clear that some causes of death could be prevented. I knew I wasn't going to be a doctor, like Mr. Wylie had hoped, but maybe I could use my writing and my platform as a poet to help save lives.

I worked on my book for months, sometimes bringing my manuscript to edit at work. One weekend Mr. Wylie went to visit his father, Daddy Mack, in South Carolina, and Brandon and I were left alone. Brandon really didn't need to stay at work with me that day because I was more than capable of handling the load. There weren't any cases on our book and we were only open in case someone called or showed up.

We were sitting in the Old Country Buffet room when surprisingly he asked me how my book was coming along. I didn't think he paid much attention to me in that way.

"Do you want to read my short story?" I asked.

He gave me a look that said not really, but he held out his hand.

Then I handed him the story and he stretched out on the floor until he was comfortable. He began to read and I watched him as he turned page after page, his facial expression changing. He was the first person to read my story, so I wondered if he would get it. I felt vulnerable, knowing he was seeing a personal part of me for the first time.

Toward the end he looked emotional.

"Wow. That was deep."

"Were you crying over there?" I could have sworn I saw a tear in his eye as he read the last page.

"Almost. It's really good. Like, really good."

"You think so?" I blushed and felt some of those same butterflies I'd felt years ago.

Not long after that, official copies of my book arrived in the mail. I wasn't scheduled to work that day, but I rushed to the funeral home to show Mr. Wylie the finished product. He was sitting behind his desk when I burst in and handed him a copy of the pink book. He took the book in his hands and leaned back in his chair.

"Hot dog!" He was excited as he examined the book. "Is this my copy?" he asked.

"Yes! Turn to the acknowledgments," I instructed him. It was taking him too long, so I walked behind his desk and found the page for him. Listed under the "Encouraging Spirits" section was "Albert P. Wylie (my godfather)." I had listed Brandon too, because he had critiqued my story.

A few weeks later, when my book was released, a reporter from the *City Paper* contacted me to write a feature for the publication. When she asked me about the best location to meet, I could think of only one place. She said she wasn't afraid at all. In fact, she thought it might add an interesting twist to her story. We did the interview in one of the arrangement rooms. She began her article:

A funeral parlor may not quite be the first place you think of when you consider finding peace and quiet. But on a warm afternoon in June, one of the city's burgeoning young poets finds just that at the Wylie Funeral Home in West Baltimore.

"I like to write in quiet spaces," says 20-year-old poet Sheri Booker, who has worked at the mortuary as an administrative assistant for the past six years.[*]

One day at the beginning of winter, only days after finishing finals at my local Catholic college, I found myself parking my Bronco in front of the funeral home even though I hadn't planned on showing up there until Wednesday when my shift began.

Ms. Angela was swamped because it was the end of the year and bodies were piled sky-high. For some reason there always seemed to be an influx of calls from Thanksgiving to New Year's Day. She told me there was one stretched out on the embalming table, one on the dressing room table, one in a casket, two in the fridge, and another one that needed to be picked up. If I had known that it was a full house, I would have stayed away. It became chaotic in times like this, especially since every case needed special attention.

With the Wylie men out on a service, the office was quiet except for the bickering between Ms. Angela and Mr. Wylie's cousin Billy. Billy was like our maintenance man. He worked six days a week doing the odd jobs of the funeral home. Though he was pushing sixty, he could pass for a young man from a distance since he was always wearing a fresh pair of Timberland boots or sneakers, a baseball cap, and a sweatshirt. Brandon often gave Billy hand-me-downs when he cleaned Brandon's room for him every Saturday.

---

[*] Felicia A. Wilks, "Liberating Rhythm," *City Paper* (Baltimore), July 2, 2003.

When I walked in, Ms. Angela was teasing him about being broke again and about not being able to eat anything because of his dentures. Cousin Billy had survived the streets, so he wasn't bothered by Ms. Angela's cheap shots. By giving him a job, Mr. Wylie was giving Billy a second chance at life. It had broken his heart that the cousin who peed the bed with him as a kid had gotten caught up in drugs, and he wanted to help him get back on his feet. As our custodian, Billy vacuumed all the rooms, swept the vestibule, folded chairs from the funeral services, and sometimes cleaned or fixed something in the embalming room or garage. Before Cousin Billy started working with us, I'd had to do many of his chores, so I really appreciated having him around.

Just as Billy was about to launch one of his comebacks at Ms. Angela, Mr. Wylie phoned in.

"Sister Bertrille just walked in," she told him. She'd always say I came to work dressed up and acting like a nun, but she knew I had on thongs beneath my habit. She loved to sass and come up with nicknames for everyone. She called one of the funeral directors who sometimes used our building "Mother" because she thought he acted like a sissy.

"Booker's there? Good!" I could hear Mr. Wylie's mouth through the phone. "Send Billy with her to pick up my body."

Mr. Wylie had just hung up with a family that insisted he pick up their loved one from another firm. That was one thing Mr. Wylie hardly ever did—he didn't want to step on anyone else's toes or do the messy job of correcting someone else's work. But this family would not back down and so he'd finally given in.

Before that afternoon, I had assisted Mr. Wylie on only

one prior removal. One day a couple of years earlier, he'd simply and abruptly said, "Meet me out front."

I followed his command and soon learned we here headed to a nearby hospital to pick up a body. When someone died at a hospital, there was a strict procedure you needed to follow. Before we were allowed to make a removal, we had to first call the hospital to make sure the body was ready to be released. Having an undertaker pick up a body from the hospital was bad for their business, so we had to wait until an orderly transported the body to the morgue. Sometimes that took a little longer than expected. There was also the issue of the death certificate. Some hospitals didn't allow the removal of the body without a signed death certificate. If this was the case, we would have to wait for the attending physician or someone else with authority to sign.

Most families called us right after they received condolences from the nursing staff or hospital chaplain. The body was still warm and might even still be connected to the machines that had struggled to keep the person alive. Sometimes it was a long process to get the body ready for us and to encourage the family to let go of their loved one's hand forever.

Calling the hospital to confirm a body's release was never easy because each hospital had a different bureaucratic system. If you called University of Maryland Medical Center, then you needed to speak with someone in pathology before you were given the go-ahead. Bon Secours or Maryland General required you to speak to security, and the on-duty officer would check his clipboard to see if the remains were ready. Other hospitals required you to speak with someone in admitting to make sure the cadaver had been flagged in the computer. That process wasn't always easy because the communication within the hospital wasn't flawless. A body could be left upstairs for hours. If a nurse forgot to flag the death in the computer, you'd call and they'd tell you that according to their medical records, the person we were looking for was good and alive in the system.

That day our body was at Bon Secours Hospital and Mr. Wylie had already called ahead to confirm it was ready to be released. Bon Secours was where most of the elderly and lower-income people went in our area for their health problems—it wasn't the best hospital for advanced medical treatment, but it worked for minor aches and pains. Mr. Wylie loaded the black Windstar minivan, which was always used for removals, with the stretcher and pulled it in front of the building. The back windows were tinted, and the ABW logo for "Albert and Brandon Wylie" was pasted on the side.

He blew the horn for me and I hopped in and strapped on my seat belt, thrilled to be invited along. The inside was as clean as a brand-new car. There were no seats in the back, just metal tracks to easily roll in the gurney. Though there was an air freshener hanging from the rearview mirror, the minivan still had a peculiar odor. It wasn't the same heavy, instantly recognizable scent of death that I had become accustomed to, but instead smelled like a sanitized version as though it had been bleached or wiped down with a cleaning spray. I had never been inside the van before, but everyone else had used it to run errands like picking up death certificates at Vital Records.

Mr. Wylie asked me to reach inside the glove compartment and hand him the laminated sign that read "Funeral

Director on Call" so that he could pull into the emergency section of the hospital drive and make the removal. We rolled up to the hospital and parked on the curve in front of the emergency room, right behind an ambulance. He handed me a pair of latex gloves and grabbed a pair for himself; then I followed him to the back of the van and together we rolled the stretcher out. We walked through the automated sliding doors and stopped at the security desk, where we were greeted by a guard who smiled at Mr. Wylie in recognition. He didn't require us to pull out the usual identification—he just called on his walkie-talkie to inform someone that he was going into the morgue for a few minutes and led us down the hallway to the inside of a chilly room.

Thank God there weren't any bodies in sight. Stainless steel drawers lined the walls of what felt like a walk-in freezer. It looked just like the rooms I had seen on television, though it felt way creepier than the basement at the funeral home because I had no idea what was inside those drawers. There was an antiseptic feeling about it, like not many living people had been inside.

I stayed close to the door, afraid of somehow being locked inside the windowless room, while the guard checked the list of names to identify the drawer number. He pulled the door open and slid out a body that was wrapped in several white sheets, as if it had been mummified. The security officer went around to the left side of the drawer while Mr. Wylie stayed on the right, and then, on Mr. Wylie's "Ready," they lifted the body up and over the open drawer and lowered it onto the gurney, strapping it and then zipping it into the bag that was attached to the stretcher. After the guard handed us the death certificate, Mr. Wylie grabbed the front end of the stretcher and told me to push. All eyes were on me as I pushed the body through the long hallway of the hospital. We rolled the body out the double doors and placed it in the van. It was that simple. Once we were back in the van, we took off our gloves and washed our hands with an antibacterial liquid. I kept washing my hands over and over again. Mission complete.

• • • •

THE removal Mr. Wylie was charging me and Cousin Billy to handle promised to be much easier than any other kind since there was no bureaucracy or grieving family to maneuver through. We were just picking up a body and transporting it from Point A to Point B. Cousin Billy could have handled it on his own, but he couldn't drive, so that's why he needed me to go with him. We probably wouldn't even be seen by anyone, which was a blessing since neither of us was dressed for a removal. I was in jeans but my overcoat shielded my casual clothing enough for me to look professional. Usually a representative from Wylie's doing a pickup was properly dressed in slacks, a tie, and a dress shirt.

"You'll need these." Billy handed me a pair of rubber gloves before we got out of the van. I wasn't expecting to do any heavy lifting, but I put the gloves on anyway. I knocked on the back door and waited for someone to answer. When no one did, I walked around to the front of the building. The receptionist assumed that I was there to view one of the bodies, since unlike us, their firm held day viewings. But I told her

I was with Wylie Funeral Home and that I was there to pick up a woman named Ms. Griffin on behalf of her family.

She called for her manager, who then escorted me into his office, where the death certificate had become lost beneath all the paper on his cluttered desk. After finding the paperwork finally, he walked me through the back hallway and into the embalming room, where the body had been prepared for removal. Along with Ms. Griffin, there were several other bodies in the room. Two were still covered by sheets, while one was fully dressed and casketed. Two morticians dressed in smocks were touching up the features of a fourth body laid out on the working table. It felt strange to be the sole representative for the Wylie Funeral Home, and even more bizarre to be in another embalming room.

Billy sat in the van waiting for my cue, and I opened the door and waved him in. I attempted to help Billy with the stretcher, but he had it under control, and then the manager helped him lift Ms. Griffin and get her into our van.

I was on the way back to the funeral home when I received a call from Ms. Angela.

"Where are you?" she asked anxiously.

"I'm on Franklin Street." I worried that I had forgotten something at the other funeral home.

"Good. Can you stop at McDonald's and get me a Big N' Tasty meal on your way back?"

"Sure," I agreed.

The noonday mix played on the radio as I sat in the lunch-hour line with cars wrapped around the double arches. Since it looked like we'd be there for a while, Billy hopped out to grab a pack of cigarettes from a neighboring gas station. I shouted my order at the intercom. When the line finally moved, I quickly whipped around the corner, but not before smashing the rear end of the minivan against the guard pole. With my bumper attached to the pole, I turned back to check on Ms. Griffin. The body bag was still intact, but my heart was racing like I had been in a head-on collision. I was embarrassed and had no idea what to do next, especially since everyone in the parking lot was staring at me. The front of my car was too close to the wall to move forward, so I thought the only way to untangle myself was to shift into reverse. Only by doing that, I smashed the rear end into the guard pole even more. The sound of crushing metal seemed to be getting louder and louder. I shifted the gears from reverse to drive, and after going back and forth I was finally able to separate the car from the pole. Again, I looked back to check on Ms. Griffin, who lay there quietly, unaware of the commotion.

The McDonald's workers from both window one and window two poked their heads out to see what all the noise was about. Embarrassed, I drove on to the first window, where I paid the cashier.

"Someone does this every day," the young worker tried to console me. Looking back through the side mirror, I saw a rainbow of car paint on the pole, but it was no consolation for my plight. I was terrified that the body in the back was not still in one piece.

When he returned, I asked Billy to take a look at the back of the car. He almost choked on his cigarette when he saw the damage. It had basically been a fender bender between my vehicle and the inappropriately placed pole, but the damage on the car looked like I had been rammed by a tractor-trailer more than once. Just looking at the car, it seemed like I should have been hauled off in an ambulance, or that a passenger in the backseat would have lost a limb.

"Thank the Lord I wasn't in here. You all right?"

That made me feel worse as I realized that I would have to take the blame all by myself. "Yes, I'm all right. I just hit the little guarder pole thingy and Mr. Wylie is going to kill me." He nodded his head in agreement.

"What should I do?"

"Call him!"

I dialed the number, hoping he was still on a service, but he answered on the first ring.

"Hey, how's your day?" I asked, trying to mask the anxiety I felt.

"Good. I'm on my way back to Gilmor Street. You got my body?"

"Um . . . you're going to fire me," I told him. I had seen people get fired for much less.

"Why? What's up?"

"I was just in an accident in the van."

"Where? Are you all right? Where's Billy?"

"He's right here. I'm fine." I cringed because I didn't want to answer the rest of his questions.

"Where's my body?"

"She's in the back, but she's fine."

"What happened? Did you call the police?"

"No, because I was the only car involved. I hit the yellow pole in the drive-through at McDonald's." I could hardly bring myself to say it aloud.

"You took my body to McDonald's?" He was still calm.

"Ms. Angela—"

"I'll call you back." He hung up abruptly.

That meant he needed to think. Brandon crashed cars all the time, but there were never human remains involved. I hated messing up and I knew I'd let him down. Was he going to take the damage out of my check? If so, I would be paying it back for years.

The next few moments seemed to go by in slow motion. We rode back to the funeral home in silence and then parked in the garage. I went upstairs to Ms. Angela's office and waited to be disciplined while Cousin Billy stayed downstairs to help get Ms. Griffin out of the van and assess the damage. Ms. Angela just kept saying, "Chile. Mm-mm."

Billy came upstairs soon, looking glum too. We all knew this was bad.

Then Ms. Angela jumped up. "Come on, Billy. Let's go eat our food before it gets cold."

Right then, Mr. Wylie called me on the intercom. "Booker, come to the basement." He wasn't happy.

I walked down and into the dressing room and stared at the wall in front of me.

"Are you sure you just hit a pole?"

"Yes. I am so sorry."

"Darn, what kind of pole was that?" He then turned to Brandon, who was still inspecting the body. "How is she?"

"Oh, she's full. She just had a Big N' Tasty meal," he joked. I gave him the evil eye. This was no time for jokes, especially not at my expense.

Brandon unzipped the bag and transferred the body to the embalming table. I hated that he was there. I didn't want him to see me reprimanded. I had spent my entire tenure trying to be perfect, and with one lapse in judgment I was realizing that I might have lost it all.

"Pop, come here. This woman doesn't have any legs."

Mr. Wylie walked over to the body and looked.

"Where are Ms. Griffin's legs?" he shouted at me, his face stern this time. Judging from the damage to both the car and the body, it wasn't a big leap to think that Ms. Griffin's legs could have been lost in the accident.

"Huh? Did you look in her bag?"

It was the first thing that came to mind. I knew I hadn't checked the body bag before leaving the other funeral home, and my mind was swirling. Nothing made sense anymore.

"Come here." He called me over.

I walked into the embalming room, and poor old Ms. Griffin was on the table legless. Instead of looking at Mr. Wylie, I stared at the wall just as I had the first time he told me to six years before. I looked for Billy; he was nowhere to be found. I was on trial all alone. Vehicular manslaughter—I had managed to kill a corpse.

Mr. Wylie and Brandon burst into laughter. They had already known that this woman was an amputee before they tormented me in the basement. Ms. Griffin had died from diabetes, which more than likely explained why she was without legs.

"What would make you take my body through the drive-through?"

"I don't know. Ms. Angela asked me to stop."

I had worked there long enough to know that you simply don't drive someone's deceased loved one through the drive-through of a fast-food restaurant. It was negligent. Later that evening, Mr. Wylie called me with an estimate of the damage—three thousand dollars' worth. But he also told me he'd see me at work on Wednesday. I offered to let him take the damages out of my check.

"That's why we have insurance," he told me, and that was the end of it.

One person who didn't care about my driving history was Cousin Billy. As long as I could drop him off in East Baltimore after our Saturday shift, he wasn't worried about how well I drove. The thing that amazed me about Billy was his ability to hum along to every song that played on the car radio during our drives together as if he had written it himself. Regardless of the genre of music, he would always pick up the melody. The only thing that could interrupt his harmonizing was a pretty woman. Many times he almost got whiplash from throwing his head around to catch a glimpse of a random pretty face. I never minded giving him a ride because he always walked to get our breakfast on Saturday mornings and I figured I owed him.

One Saturday morning, I noticed that Billy was rather slow in his cleaning rituals. I asked if he was feeling well enough to go out to get breakfast and he said he felt fine. A few weeks earlier, he had taken a serious beating from a gang of boys who robbed him of his money and jewelry. Ever since the assault he hadn't been the same, but though he had been to the hospital several times, they couldn't find anything wrong with him.

I locked up the funeral home at two o'clock. Billy didn't look well when he got in my car. He complained of stomach pains and asked me to wait while he ran inside to the bathroom. After almost twenty minutes of sitting outside, I went to look for him. Billy was sitting on the stairs crying, and suddenly he upchucked a pool of blood. The floor was covered in it. I grabbed the trash can for him and ran to the intercom to call Brandon, who was in the basement embalming.

When Brandon came upstairs and saw the trail of blood in the hallway, we called 911. Billy continued to sit on the stairs and cry. He told us how scared he was, and we were also terrified for him.

The ambulance came and got Billy quickly to the closest hospital, which was Maryland General. We watched Billy off and then we shared a hug, devastated by what we had just seen. Brandon cleaned up the mess and I drove home worried to death about what would happen next. But Mr. Wylie, who was out of town when this happened, called me later that night to let me know that Billy was just fine. When I called Billy at the hospital myself, he was in great spirits and we laughed and joked. He told me the hospital planned to run further tests the next day. But a day later, we lost Billy.

I couldn't help but think that Billy had known his fate that afternoon on the stairs.

At Wylie's, we understood the importance of treating each case as if it were our own mother or father or sibling. But though that was officially our mantra, it really hit home for us all in a different way when we had to bury one of our own. The only thing we could do was what we were used to doing on any other day: Use laughter to stop our tears. While we worked on the arrangements in the days after Billy's death, we'd tell stories: Mr. Wylie remembered how Billy peed the bed as a boy; Brandon remembered how hard he'd worked and how he'd cleaned his room until it was spotless; Ms. Angela talked about all of their silly arguments; and I reminisced about those breakfasts we'd had together.

Even with the wonderful memories, we dreaded the day we had to bury him. I read one of my poems at his funeral. Brandon's best friend sang Sam Cooke's "A Change Is Gonna Come," which brought tears to the eyes of every person who was squeezed into the small chapel. Mr. Wylie stayed in the basement, embalming the entire time, avoiding all the emotion. He left it to Brandon to give a tribute to Billy and his years at the funeral home.

After Billy's death, strange things began to happen around the funeral home. I was sitting alone one evening and I noticed that one of the internal telephone lines lit up on its own. I couldn't tell which room it was coming from, but I was sure no one else was in the building. I looked out the window to make sure Mr. Wylie's car wasn't outside—he'd slipped under my radar a few times in the past.

Spooked, I called Mr. Wylie on his cell phone and he assured me that no one was in the building. Then I made an all-call on the intercom to be absolutely positive I was alone. No one answered. I began a room-by-room search of the building. When I got to the downstairs bathroom, the door seemed to be locked, which meant that someone had to have locked it from the inside. I ran upstairs, grabbed my purse and keys, and ran out the door, leaving every light on, the computer on, and the door unlocked. I didn't go back that night, and Mr. Wylie had to come back to lock up. It was the first time I'd ever felt afraid to be alone in the funeral home. Days later, I started thinking that Cousin Billy might have been sending a sign through the phone and that he was just checking in on us.

A few months after I had my fright, one of our drivers, Kevin, swore Cousin Billy appeared sitting next to him while he was backing the van into the garage. Kevin came back in the building with a knot on his head from where he'd bumped it on the window after being startled by Billy's ghost.

I'd never seen a ghost, but I did believe in spirits, because Billy's wasn't the first I'd encountered. A few months after she died, I felt Aunt Mary's presence at home. I was sitting on the bed in the room that used to be hers, and then—*kaboom*—her picture fell from the wall. That was the first time Aunt Mary tried to get my attention. The next time she showed up, the upstairs toilet decided to flush on its own. Out of nowhere, we heard the unmistakable *swish*. We were all home together and just looked at one another. My mother said it first: "Hi, Aunt Mary." I wasn't scared; I just felt comforted to know she was still watching over us. And now we had Cousin Billy to protect us at the funeral home.

CHAPTER

TWELVE

"**THIS** is it," Mr. Wylie told me as he pulled over to the side of the road and parked on an empty piece of dirt. His freshly buffed tires were now covered in dust, but he wasn't worried. They'd look brand-new before the funeral the next morning.

"Is someone buried here?" I joked, yet unsure.

"This is where I'm going to build our new funeral home."

"Really?!"

"Come on . . ." He hopped out of his car and walked over to open my door. My high heels sunk into the earth as I walked around. Mr. Wylie was a visionary, and he saw what I couldn't at the time: a booming business. The property was located on the busy Liberty Road corridor of Baltimore County outside the city. It didn't look like the place for the plans he had shown me; it looked like a piece of dirt, probably an eyesore to the neighboring homes on the left and right.

"I already bought it." He handed me the deed to the land, which was now his. He had been driving up Liberty Road one day when he heard the Lord speak to him and tell him that residents of Baltimore County needed a funeral home in their area so that they wouldn't have to travel back and forth into the city to make funeral arrangements. He started looking for a place to build a new branch, but there didn't seem to be the right property for sale, one that was large enough for his vision and zoned for business. The Liberty Road property was perfect but wasn't zoned properly. So every day for the last few months, Mr. Wylie had driven to this location, walked around, and prayed to one day own it. He knew he needed a much bigger faith to turn that land into a funeral home from the ground up, but he wanted this for all of us, especially Brandon, who would be graduating with a business degree in the spring and would be able to operate the business on his own.

It hadn't been easy to secure the property. After months of hearings and debates, he was finally awarded the permits to build a new funeral home. In the end, his triumph was historic. It would be the first African American facility built in that area.

Mr. Wylie was careful to follow all the proper procedures in acquiring the land, but in all his excitement, he had prematurely shown his plans to another funeral director. Before he could even finish building, that funeral director partnered with a white firm to bring in a rival business. The location they planned was going to be only a few blocks away from our new branch. But that didn't deter Mr. Wylie; it only motivated him to be bigger and better.

The new funeral home was a major multimillion-dollar business deal that promised a state-of-the-art facility, and I was going along for the ride. Since I was still contemplating law school, Mr. Wylie kept me close to the business deals. I tried to keep up as he worked with lawyers, contractors, and developers. He asked me to draft all his communications, and he saved all the incoming documents for me to read.

By this point, Mr. Wylie trusted my judgment when it came to business. When my best friend from high school needed to make a few extra dollars for her trip abroad, I asked Mr. Wylie if she could work for him, and she began working the next day. He had no hesitation bringing me into his personal affairs either. One afternoon, he called me into his office and told me he had changed his will. I couldn't imagine why he was telling me this and even wondered if he had added me into it. But it turned out that he wanted to tell me that Brandon would inherit the original funeral home and his wife would inherit the new one. I guess he was looking for some kind of validation for something he knew he couldn't share with anyone else. Even though I wasn't in his will, I still envisioned owning one of the firms one day. I imagined that I would marry Brandon and we would run the funeral homes together—only after he had grown up and I had written more books and traveled the world.

At the end of the summer we broke ground, and the project was on its way.

· · · ·

IF Al Wylie decided he didn't want something anymore, he just got rid of it. That included clothes, furniture, cars, and even employees. Everything was disposable to him. For the first seven years that I worked at the funeral home, we used a company called Stacker Caskets. Stacker provided all our minimum metal caskets, simple caskets that came in silver or bronze for families on a budget, and each week we ordered at least five or six. The casket company provided all the notepads in the office. We even had coffee mugs with the Stacker logo. But when Stacker did not support the National Funeral Directors and Morticians Association at their annual conference, which took place in Baltimore that year, Mr. Wylie cut all ties with them immediately. He felt that since so many black funeral homes used their products, they could at least sponsor the biggest African American funeral industry organization in the country. The day after the conference ended, Mr. Wylie had me print out a sign to post on the bulletin board to explain that we would no longer use Stacker Casket Company and we would use Warfield-Rohr products instead. But in what I considered his most drastic measure, he also crossed their name and number out of the sacred green book.

Similarly, we had to ban one of our drivers, Charles, from the green book after he used one of the funeral home's limousines to pick up his son from school. Mr. Wylie called an impromptu staff meeting during which he warned us not to contact Charles to drive for any service; if we did we would be fired too. He took the black Magic Marker and crossed Charles's name and phone number out, and we could never make out the numbers again. Both Stacker Caskets and Charles made appeals to Mr. Wylie, but he never budged.

I wasn't sure if Mr. Wylie's zero-tolerance policy was a good business policy or if he incorporated what he had learned on the streets to run his funeral home. But he could be ruthless and stubborn, and that attitude could spill over into his treatment of his employees too.

"Leave my key." Those words stung like a bee. No explanation. No conversation. Those were the words you heard when your services were no longer needed at Wylie Funeral Home. That's if you were there long enough to even earn a key.

If Mr. Wylie was really disgusted with you, then he'd let Ms. Angela give you the news. "He said leave his key," she'd say with no remorse. Or she would hand you your last paycheck and instruct you not to return the next day.

I had watched this scene play out so many times over the years. It seemed as if the moment I felt a connection to an apprentice, driver, or evening employee, they were removed from the staff directory and their name went into the urn on the kitchen table, now overflowing with the names of employees who had passed through.

There was an apprentice named Jackie that everyone liked, but she could never find a babysitter, so Mr. Wylie asked her not to come back. Then there was Chanel II, who was a thick, dark-skinned woman, the complete opposite of the first Chanel. Her husband made her quit because he thought her schedule was too demanding. And of course we still missed the original Chanel, who we all wished would return one day. Except for those few, we remembered our former co-workers only by certain characteristics they had. There was "the girl with the tongue ring," who lasted only a week until Mr. Wylie discovered her piercing, and "the soldier boy," a friend's son who had returned from the army but didn't like taking orders from Mr. Wylie. I hated to see new people come because I knew that they would inevitably be leaving us soon. And because

Brandon, Ms. Angela, and I were all loyal to Mr. Wylie, we treated those people just like he did. If he was completely over them, then so were we. If he gave them a second chance, we did too.

The girl from my high school, Tuverla, ended up working for us at one point. Then one afternoon she got caught in the rain while picking up a death certificate from the Division of Vital Records. She did what any black woman without an umbrella would have done: wrapped a scarf around her hair so it wouldn't get wet. The supervisor from DVR called Mr. Wylie and complained about her lack of professionalism in representing him with a rag on her head. He fired Tuverla as soon as she got back.

The average tenure of a Wylie Funeral Home employee was two to six weeks, tops. Ms. Angela and I were the exception to the rule. We were both in our seventh year and the only non-blood staff members who had made it that long. We were consistent and loyal. I was certain that the two of us would die working there.

• • • •

I decided that I would take six months off after college graduation. I wanted to travel, study for the LSAT, and apply to a few journalism programs. For the first time, I realized that I was ready to leave Baltimore. My mother was healthier and I started to believe that she would outlive us all. A few years before, I wasn't sure if she'd make it to see me graduate from high school, but she had lived to see me graduate from college too. Her survival challenged what I'd started to accept: that my life had to revolve around death. So I began searching for out-of-state graduate schools. I had my heart set on attending a journalism program in Chicago in the beginning of the year and I had Mr. Wylie's full support.

Then everything changed. Ms. Angela came in one day and told us that she had to have a biopsy done and needed to be off for a week. She asked me to cover her shift. No one wanted to admit it, but we were all concerned about Angela. She was truly Mr. Wylie's right hand when it came to day-to-day operations. For the last seven years, she'd made sure that he had to be concerned only with embalming and directing funerals. She took care of the rest.

During my first two years working at the funeral home, Ms. Angela never took a vacation. If she was sick, she would come in and answer the phones. I remember her even coming to pick me up on snow days, since when the schools were closed the funeral home was still open. So whether she was going to be gone because she had a health problem or she just needed some leisure time, in my eyes, she deserved every hour and more.

Mr. Wylie called me the night before Ms. Angela was to return to work. He hadn't heard from her and was beginning to grow suspicious.

"Do you think Angela had a biopsy?" he asked me over the phone.

"Yes. I don't think she'd lie about something like that."

"She hasn't answered any of my calls all week." He sounded really worried about her. In seven years, he hadn't gone this long without talking to her. "I called her son and he didn't know anything about the surgery."

I told him that maybe she didn't tell her children about the biopsy because she didn't want to alarm them. Maybe she told only the family that she knew could handle it: her family at Wylie Funeral Home. My mother hadn't told anyone about her sickness until after the fact, so the idea of Ms. Angela acting the same way didn't seem too strange to me.

But the following morning when Ms. Angela arrived at work, Mr. Wylie was standing at the front door with a box in his arms containing all her belongings: every pair of shoes that had accumulated under her desk for the last seven years, all the mismatched earrings that had covered her desk because she had the tendency to remove the one on her right ear when she talked on the phone, the pictures of her children she'd taped to the cabinet above her desk. He'd even thrown in the cheap pair of stockings that she'd bought from the corner store.

As I stood watching, he simply handed the box to her and asked for his key. She stared at him but then slowly removed it from her key ring and put it on the register stand without saying a word. Then she took her box and disappeared.

The way he'd banished Ms. Angela so rashly was completely unlike Mr. Wylie, and he wasn't the same after she left. As for me and Brandon, it felt like our parents were going through a bitter divorce. Since we stayed with our father, our allegiance was to him—we erased Angela's name from our vocabulary and never mentioned her to him again.

Later in the week, Mr. Wylie called and asked if I could cover the daytime shift until he found someone else. I'd never filled in for Ms. Angela before, though it was a moment they had been preparing me for all these years. But I couldn't help but wonder what Mr. Wylie was capable of. If he'd cut Ms.

Angela loose so coldly, what would he do to me? The moment I sat behind Ms. Angela's desk, I was no longer Mr. Wylie's pupil—I was now his full-time employee. Before I could even get comfortable in my chair, he had a list of tasks for me to complete.

It was clear that Ms. Angela had been the glue that kept everything together; we'd soon discover that it took all three of us to do her job. While I had thought I had learned everything there was to know about funeral service, I realized I had no idea how much Ms. Angela had handled on her own. I knew very little about filing insurance claims and handling veterans' services, and embarrassingly enough, I didn't even know how to type a death certificate on the typewriter. Brandon had to teach me. I was too proud to accept help at first and questioned everything he showed me. "Are you sure it doesn't go like this?" I'd say, or "Mr. Wylie does it like that." Sometimes it felt like hollering and screaming was the only way for us to communicate. But we stopped after we realized that Mr. Wylie was just going to leave it up to us to run things in his absence. Most mornings he had site meetings with the developers, which kept him away for hours at a time. And when it wasn't a morning meeting, it was an afternoon zoning hearing, or a meeting with the community organization, since they were still resistant to the project. The two homes next door did not want the traffic of a funeral home to become a part of their daily life—not to mention that the idea of living next to one was just plain creepy. Before Mr. Wylie could be approved to build, he had to meet with the traffic light services to get a signal put in place. There was financing and vending, contracts and landscapes, architects and designers. He was swamped.

In his absence, Brandon and I did everything related to the business as a team—he let me drive his Mercedes to run errands; together we talked to the families making arrangements. And we gossiped and chatted and joked, the way good friends did. During our moments alone, we sometimes talked about the stress Mr. Wylie was clearly under. You could feel the tension he was carrying whenever he came into the room, and we wondered if that was the real reason behind his firing of Ms. Angela.

One morning during our usual breakfast together, Brandon told me he wasn't sure if he wanted to do funeral business for the rest of his life.

"Like you have a choice," I said, pointing out that his father was building a new funeral home for him to run. He just shrugged.

Working so closely with Brandon brought back some of the butterflies I'd felt around him when I'd first started at the funeral home as such a young girl. I'd been ten years old when I wrote his name in my diary and dreamed of becoming his girlfriend. But over the years, I realized what an immature, silly boy he was, and all of my feelings for him disappeared. Now, seven and a half years later, we had become closer.

Everyone was nervous in the weeks leading up to the grand opening of the new facility. It almost seemed unreal that the piece of dirt that Mr. Wylie had walked across and prayed on was now a huge funeral home, one that would make history. It was an enormous occasion that would complete a lifelong mission for Mr. Wylie.

Before the opening, Mr. Wylie had searched for new staff for the facility. He wanted an additional funeral director who would be able to bounce between both locations, and he hoped to find a woman to fill the position. A few years back, he'd met a young woman at the National Funeral Directors Association convention, an annual gathering for funeral directors, vendors, and students who were looking to begin their careers. After ignoring follow-up messages from her back then, he now decided to give her a phone interview. He liked what he heard when they reconnected. In the years since they'd first spoken, she had already graduated from mortuary school and passed the National Board exam, but she was working in a shoe store in Atlanta because no funeral home was willing to hire her full-time.

After she passed the phone interview, Mr. Wylie flew her in to meet with him in person. I thought she looked like a teenager, but when I got to know her more I realized her personality was strong enough to balance her look. She passed Mr. Wylie's tests during the services she went on with him, and so at the end of her weekend stay he offered her a position that met her salary requirements. She would move to Baltimore at the end of the year and be an integral part of the new business.

I felt that Mr. Wylie had made his decision too quickly, since I knew he had not tested her skills in the basement. Could she embalm or prep a body? Mr. Wylie ignored my reservations and said vehemently that it didn't matter—she was teachable. Just days before the New Year she moved to the city alone, but it took only a week and a half for Mr. Wylie to realize that once again I was dead-on. She had remarkable book knowledge but not enough hands-on experience. At the end of her second week he gave her two weeks' pay and sent her back down south.

I convinced him to rehire Tuverla. She was already licensed, which made her the pick of the litter. Most women in the field would rather direct the services and make arrangements, but

Tuverla was the exact opposite. If she could stay in the basement all day, she would.

While I was excited about the new venture, I also felt slighted that Mr. Wylie didn't offer me the position at the new funeral home. I knew he couldn't send his two best people to the new facility, but in my eyes it was about the principle, and he should have at least discussed it with me.

It felt bittersweet opening the new building without Ms. Angela. She deserved to be there. The day before the grand opening, all the staff had to report to the new funeral home for a briefing on the procedures for the special event. Of course everything had to be perfect, including every piece of hair on our heads. Since we had a long night and early morning in front of us, I asked Brandon if I could sleep over at his place that night. He lived two minutes away, compared to the thirty-five minutes that it would take me to drive home that night and then again the next morning. So I packed an overnight bag.

We were already into the next day when we finished the preparations. Brandon slipped me his house keys and told me that he'd be right behind me. It wasn't that we were being sneaky, but we figured no one needed to know that I was sleeping over at his place. We didn't want anyone to draw any conclusions.

By the time I arrived, I was exhausted. I had time to snoop around his place a little before he arrived, and of course I was curious, but I didn't want to betray his trust, so I kept myself out of the bedroom. From the looks of things in the front rooms, Brandon was keeping his place up pretty nice. Everything was spotless except for the ashes that littered the table from his cigar.

When Brandon got home, he crashed beside me on the sofa. "Do you need anything? Are you thirsty?" he asked. He was treating me like a guest, and I couldn't help but be impressed.

"No, thanks. I do want to shower, though," I replied.

He grabbed a towel from the linen closet and set up the shower for me. When I got out, he was still in the living room watching television, so I went into the bedroom and sat on his bed. It felt so soft that I just wanted to melt away. After a few minutes, he came in and placed his watch on the dresser with the others in his collection and then grabbed a pillow to go out into the living room.

"Are you sleeping on the couch?" I asked.

"Where else am I going to sleep?"

"This is your bed. You could have made me sleep on the couch." I smiled.

"Nah." He headed out into the living room.

"You can sleep in here with me. I won't bite." I was nervous, but I trusted him.

"Are you sure?"

"Yes." I rolled my eyes.

He changed into his pajamas and got into bed.

"Can you believe that we're opening a new funeral home tomorrow?" I asked.

"I know. That's crazy."

"And it's your joint."

"Yeah, it's my joint. It's *my* joint." He said the words back to me as if he had only just realized that on Monday morning he'd really be in charge. I could hear the fear and excitement in his voice. If his father gave him total control, he would have to prove himself as a man, a businessman.

"Yup! And you know you only get one chance at funeral service," I teased.

Somehow we drifted closer to each other in bed and I found myself cradled under his arm. It felt like the safest place in the world.

The next morning, all seemed right with the world, and I felt so much pride about the moment I was about to witness as we made our way to the opening.

The weatherman was calling for snow that January morning, but Mr. Wylie had every intention of moving forward with his unveiling. He had specifically scheduled our grand opening for the weekend of Dr. Martin Luther King's birthday. The sky was a bit gray, but we were prepared to open our doors to the hundreds of guests that had been invited. They arrived dressed for the occasion, many in full length minks and long dress coats, and the church folk had pulled out their fancy hats and gloves. There were so many familiar faces in the crowd, including families that we had worked with, our church members, family, and friends. Some local politicians and businessmen also gathered outside with the rest of the crowd as we all waited for Mr. Wylie to cut the red ribbon to officially open the building.

After the ceremony, we escorted our guests into the large chapel for a brief gathering. This was the moment we had all been waiting for. Mr. Wylie got up. In his remarks he thanked everyone from the contractors and the lawyers to Brandon and his wife. But he forgot to thank his staff. The newer staff I could understand, but I was family, and I couldn't believe he didn't acknowledge all the afternoons I'd spent listening to him talk about his grand plans, all the letters I'd drafted and the phone calls I'd made on behalf of the project. I'd made this day happen too.

We were so busy at the opening that I didn't talk to Brandon all day. He had been posing for pictures and speaking with reporters. I didn't even say good-bye to anyone before I left that afternoon. The whole event had lost its sheen.

When I got to work on Monday, Brandon wasn't there. He was sitting in his brand-new office across town, hoping for a death call to come in. We had an in-house funeral that morning, and out of habit, I sat by the window waiting for his Mercedes to pull up. Every time I heard the front door open, I expected to hear his footsteps coming up the stairs. That's when I realized that he wasn't coming back.

CHAPTER
THIRTEEN

SNOWFLAKES began to cascade from the sky. One by one they fell until the snow covered my car windshield. The school across the street had already dismissed its students, and I still had an hour left in my shift. I kept watching from my window, and though it was beautiful, I wanted it to stop, because I knew that no matter how many inches accumulated or how messy the streets became, the funeral home would still be open the next day. We never shut our doors for business because of the weather; only cemeteries did. If a couple of feet of snow were on the ground, it would have to be plowed before a plot could be dug, so we'd postpone the service. But as long as the government hadn't declared a snow emergency, we had to show up at work.

I also wanted the snow to stop because I didn't want to have to clean off my car in the skirt and pumps I was wearing. Plus,

I did not need Jack Frost nibbling at my fingertips if I was going to be at work typing death certificates the next day. Brandon showed up just before quitting time, dressed sharply in his trench coat and leather Coach bucket hat. When Brandon first wore his Coach hat to work, Mr. Wylie loved it so much that I went out and bought him one for Christmas, and now they both wore them out on services. Relieved he'd shown up, I figured Brandon could clean my car since he was already wet from the burial he was returning from, but I should have known better. This was Brandon we were talking about; he had never even cleaned off his own car.

"What's up, Ri?" he greeted me as he walked into the office.

"Don't you want to clean off my car for me? I have on a skirt." I got right to the point.

"No. Get Kevin to do it."

"He's not here."

He shrugged his shoulders.

As he sat across from me, I thought about how much I missed having him around the office. I hadn't let myself pine after him too much, but I also couldn't stop thinking about the night we'd spent together. His absence had only made my feelings grow more confusing. Since he'd become the boss at the new building, I had become the unofficial boss at Gilmor Street. Even though Tuverla was licensed, she wasn't ready to take the reins yet. And I wasn't sure that I'd give them to her.

Brandon relented and agreed to clean the snow from my car on his way out, and just like that, he was gone again. But that night when I got home from work, his name popped up on my caller ID. Since he had never called me outside work before,

I worried that it was some kind of emergency, but when I picked up he said he was in an office supply store and he was just calling to see what supplies he needed for the new location. He kept me on the line as he walked around the store, and as the seconds passed I suddenly knew I needed to gather the courage to tell him how I felt about him. I knew he was in an on-again-off-again relationship with a girl at his college, and I'd heard they were off again. Maybe it was finally time to make my move.

At the time I knew nothing about being in love, but I had definitely learned that life didn't last long enough for you to stay quiet about your feelings for someone. Far too often, I'd overheard sad stories of people who waited until it was too late to confess their true emotions to the person they loved and then were left whispering sweet nothings into deaf ears. They desperately wished they'd gotten just one last hug or kiss, but they had to settle for pressing their lips to a cold cheek. I promised myself that I wasn't going to leave this earth without letting someone I really cared about know it.

I took a breath and finally slipped out the words "I think I like you" before I could stop them.

There was a deafening silence on the other end. The only sound I could hear was the deep gulp of my pride. I was all out there, totally exposed. I took the phone away from my ear to be sure we were still connected, and I saw that the clock was continuing to time the number of minutes we'd been on the line. Brandon's awkward pause reminded me of something his father would do. He was thinking.

"I think I like you too," he finally replied.

I felt a rush, and my heart wanted to jump out of my chest.

The words were ambiguous, but knowing he felt the same way was good enough for me. For years, we had hid behind jokes and sarcasm. Now we were in like—whatever that meant.

When Brandon came around, we snuck hugs and kisses, but I would always throw in a couple of punches for old times' sake, and just in case Mr. Wylie walked in. Everyone else knew what was going on, even Mr. Wylie's wife, Ms. Charleen, who was actually excited about the prospect of me officially becoming her daughter-in-law. I would have told Mr. Wylie because I felt like Brandon and I were for real, but Mr. Wylie was always out of the building, and by the time he returned I'd be gone for the day. When I told my friends and family about Brandon, they weren't surprised at all. And when I told Ms. Angela, whom I had started talking to again from time to time, she reacted as I knew she would, saying, "It's about damn time! Y'all do it yet?"

· · · ·

ANOTHER month passed and Brandon and I were still just teasing and flirting, but as time passed, I wanted more. The timing wasn't working out perfectly—it was turning out to be a busy and stressful time for both of us. My mom's cancer had found its way out of remission, and she was undergoing radiation therapy. For the first time in years we had discussed her health, and it only came up by accident. She had taken off her jacket and forgotten that she had large Xs from the blue dye that had been injected into her skin where the radiation would be performed, and when I asked her about the strange markings, she had no choice but to tell me what was going on. Somehow, I'd convinced myself that not talking about the disease had made it go away. I was devastated to be reminded that she was still so sick.

Meanwhile, Brandon had his hands full running Liberty Road. It's difficult dating a funeral director. They're like doctors—always on call. The little time we'd seen each other had started to make everything feel awkward. It felt like he was holding back, like he had to think hard before he talked to me.

So we planned a real date a week in advance to be sure that we would both be able to make the time. I was so excited to spend real time with him now that everything was different and our feelings were out in the open.

When the night finally arrived, he took me to a restaurant not far from where he lived. We sat across from each other and talked about everything from sports to politics to religion and of course work. This was the first time that I had really seen him outside his comfort zone. He was always Brandon Wylie—Mr. Wylie's son. That night, he was B.

It was getting late and we had both had a few glasses of wine. We went back to his place to continue our conversation. Neither of us knew when we'd be able to do this again. It didn't take long before we were touching each other.

He knew the human anatomy all too well. His kisses breathed life into me, causing my blood to rush through my veins. I felt chills tingle in my spine. His hands were his only instruments and they were sharp. He took them both and started at my neck. He parted them like he was making a Y incision and traced them over my body, stopping beneath my belly button. Then he used his tongue to wash me down.

We lay there imitating the corpses we saw daily. Breathless. Still. Silent. Unaware of the world around us.

Just like any man on the clock, Brandon soon got up to check his phone for missed calls. There were at least fifty missed calls and a slew of messages in the queue. Half were from his best friend, the other half from the girl he had been seeing. He dialed his best friend back to see what the emergency was all about.

"Is everything okay?" I could tell from the look on his face that something was wrong.

"She's on her way."

"Who?" I asked.

Much to his surprise, his hot-and-cold girlfriend, Janelle, suspected that he had someone at his apartment that night since he wasn't picking up his phone and was en route there with her best friend. It wasn't long before we realized she'd already arrived.

"Open this door, Brandon! I know you're in there! And I can hear her too!" she yelled as she pounded her angry fists on the front door of his first-floor apartment.

Boom. Now she was kicking the door. Then it was quiet again as she ran around the building to the patio door. That door was glass, and I expected to hear it shattering at any minute.

I did not know how I was going to escape this, but I knew I couldn't let her see me, because at the end of the day Brandon and I still had to work together. According to Brandon's best friend, who was now outside the apartment, Janelle had rounded up her sorority sisters and even some of Brandon's fraternity brothers and had them positioned around the entire complex. There was no way to escape.

"What are we going to do?" I whispered.

"I don't know," he said.

I called a good friend, Kee, who weighed about eighty pounds; I knew she couldn't fight her way in to save me, but she was an engineer and if anyone could manufacture an escape route, she could. Kee sprang into action and was at the building in ten minutes, having sped through what was usually a thirty-minute drive across town. On the way she called Brandon's best friend and they devised a plan. He would create a diversion to lure all the lookouts to the front while she pulled her car into the next complex behind Brandon's house. When they gave me the cue, I would escape through the patio door. I was terrified. The plan seemed too risky, but there was nothing else to do.

I took off my shoes and put them in my purse while I waited for the call, then took a deep breath, trying to ready myself. When we got the cue, I dashed out the door and down the hill faster than I had ever run in my life. I even ended up rolling some of the way. I hopped in the car door Kee had opened for me and we were off. I knew my car was still parked outside his complex but figured I would just have to worry about that later.

The next day I called in sick to recuperate, but I returned to work the following day as if nothing had happened. Brandon had helped me pick up my car after the great escape, but we hadn't talked since then. I was still trying to play catch-up from the day of work that I had missed. We had new death calls and old cases that needed my attention.

But just before my shift ended that Friday, a phone call came in for me. It was Brandon's girlfriend, Janelle. Apparently, Brandon had decided to tell her that the mystery woman was me after all.

After I hung up the phone with her, I walked around the corner to Mr. Wylie's office, where I could use the phone in private. I closed the office door, sat down in his big chair, and dialed Brandon's number.

"Hey. Why is she calling me?"

"Who?"

"You know who!"

"I don't know."

"What did you tell her?"

"I told her it was you."

I dropped the phone. He couldn't possibly be that stupid. Did he not understand that I rolled down a hill and ran bare-foot through an apartment complex to protect my identity?

"You told her it was me? And why on earth would you do that?"

"To make the situation better."

I was flabbergasted. Brandon had never had much common sense, something I had forgotten once my feelings got the best of me. He could have told her it was his neighbor on the third floor, or he even could have told her she was crazy since I'd been long gone when he'd finally let her in. Men lied all the time. But he'd chosen to protect her feelings over mine. I felt betrayed; I was in love with him. He had to lose something, and it had to be me.

It would be four weeks before I saw him again. Little did I know that Mr. Wylie had gotten a whiff of the situation and had forbidden him to come to Gilmor Street. When Janelle had called all her friends, she had also called Mr. Wylie at home, at two A.M. no less, to let him know too that Brandon was cheating on her. After she found out he'd been cheating with me, she'd actually called Mr. Wylie back to tell him herself.

One afternoon Brandon had no choice but to come to Gilmor Street to pick up a death certificate he needed. He walked into my office and, without a word, searched on my desk for the paper. I gave him a mug so mean that my face started to hurt.

"I'm sorry," he blurted out.

"I don't respect weak men," I told him. "You really hurt me."

"I miss you." His eyes looked sad. I wanted to forgive him right then, but I couldn't.

I called my pastor to consult with him about the situation. Even he'd heard the story from Janelle already, since she was a member of our church. I was mortified. He told me there was only one thing that I could do, and that was find a new job. But I didn't listen.

FOURTEEN

MY eighth year at Wylie's was intense. The new funeral home in Baltimore County had not caught on the way that we'd anticipated, but the calls at Gilmor Street were overwhelming. We had to schedule three viewings for one afternoon because all the families wanted a Friday burial, which meant they all had to have their viewings on Thursday. Three viewings at once was unusual, and to make things more chaotic, all three of the deceased were older women.

Mr. Wylie laid out the floor plan before the women were brought upstairs so that we were all crystal clear on who was going where. A woman named Ms. Braxton would be placed in the front room. A few days earlier, Kevin, our apprentice at the time, had picked her up from a nursing home. She was on the dressing room table when he ran upstairs to my office.

"That lady downstairs has a penis! I think I have the wrong

person, but her toe tag says Braxton," he said. I rushed down to see for myself.

Ms. Braxton was in the center of the room covered with a sheet. Her face was very hollow and thin, but her feet, which were sticking out beneath the sheet, were swollen like gigantic balloons. Kevin was right; her toe tag read "Mary Braxton." But when he lifted up the sheet, to my surprise what looked like a penis lay between her legs. I moved closer, trying to put my hand on it, but Kevin smacked me away.

"Don't touch that," he said with scolding eyes; I wasn't wearing gloves. I put some on and got close enough to give her a real inspection, sticking my hand between her legs where the alleged penis was. Now that I was only about six inches away, it didn't look that big at all. I was able to find her labia, and so I concluded that she was indeed a woman with a very inflamed clitoris.

Regardless of her gender, Ms. Braxton's family had spent the most money, so they received the front viewing room, which was the most spacious of the three. After all, Ms. Braxton was in a high-end Primrose casket, and the other women were in lower-grade caskets, and she commanded the most flower baskets and standing sprays.

Ms. McClain, one of the other women on view that day, was positioned in the middle room, the smallest. Her floral arrangements numbered only a tenth of Ms. Braxton's. In the back room, Ms. Johnson, the third body, lay neat and petite in her pink shroud and pink-and-white casket.

Only Kevin, Mr. Wylie, and I were there that day; Tuverla had the day off. At a few minutes after four, while flowers were still piling up for Ms. Braxton, Ms. Johnson's family arrived. I was in a meeting with the printer in the conference room, laying out the obituary for another service, when they arrived.

Suddenly, I heard an eruption from the back visitation room.

"That's not my mother. That is not my fucking mother!" Ms. Johnson's daughter yelled as family members agreed. I ran in and tried to console her. This was something I'd heard many times. Many people find it hard to recognize their family members when they are lying in a casket, and denial is just a part of the grieving process.

Mr. Wylie came to greet them and attempt to quiet them, but Ms. Johnson's daughter was so adamant about that not being her mother that he had to take her seriously.

He walked them into the middle room where Ms. McClain lay and asked, "Is this your mother?"

"No! Y'all better find my fucking mother."

It took us a few moments to realize what must have happened. If neither of those women was Ms. Johnson, then we must have gotten the wrong body from the hospital. We settled the Johnson family in the arrangement room and I offered them coffee. Then we retreated quickly to my office. We pulled out photographs and tried to compare them in our minds to the women downstairs. We retraced all our moves from the time we picked up the bodies from the hospital, and it seemed like we had followed the right protocol, so we figured it must have been Johns Hopkins's mistake.

Mr. Wylie dialed the hospital. It was late in the afternoon, so of course personnel were scarce and he was on hold for a long time. While we waited, our hearts and brains raced. Did we embalm the wrong body? And if that wasn't in fact Ms.

Johnson, then where was Ms. Johnson's body? She had died on Sunday and it was now Thursday. Five days was a long time in our business. She could have been cremated or buried by now by another funeral home, or even worse, brought to the Anatomy Board by mistake.

In the meantime, Ms. Johnson's daughter had called the local media and they were en route. Then the doorbell rang and Ms. Braxton's family came in to view their mother. We wondered if there was going to be yet another angry family, but they were very pleased with everything, which was a huge relief.

Last but not least, about twenty of Ms. McClain's family members strolled in to pay respect to their mother and grandmother. I walked them into the room holding the earth-tone casket with their loved one and then left to calm myself and catch my breath in the midst of the chaos. When I returned, her son looked at me and said the words I dreaded: "That ain't my mother!" I felt like I'd been hit in the stomach, but I managed to excuse myself politely and run upstairs to tell Mr. Wylie that there was yet another family denying that the body we had was the right one.

"You lying!" he yelled, disgusted. He had the telephone stuck to one ear and a lit cigarette in his hand. We were both in shock and completely unsure about what to do next—nothing like this had ever happened before. Mr. Wylie's obsession with every detail had made sure of it. I sat down at the kitchen table, trying to regroup and think through a new plan. Maybe the woman in the back room was Ms. McClain. Mr. Wylie came downstairs and walked the McClain family into the room where Ms. Johnson lay.

"Is this your mother?" he asked.

The McClain son walked up to the casket and looked at the woman carefully.

"Yes, that's our mother," he said, still angry and glaring. There she was, in strange clothes, with a completely new hairstyle, in a casket that he had not chosen.

It turned out that Ms. McClain was lying in Ms. Johnson's Misty Rose casket, wearing Ms. Johnson's shroud. It was a relief to know that Ms. McClain was safe, but we still had to solve the mystery of what had happened to Ms. Johnson.

By that time Fox 45 news was outside and Ms. Johnson's daughter was ready for her moment in the spotlight. In front of the funeral home, with the camera lights gleaming bright, she began her performance.

"Oh my God! I came to Wylie Funeral Home to view Mama and Mama is not here! There is somebody lying in Mama's casket with Mama's clothes on, but it ain't Mama. I don't know where my mama is. All I know is that Johns Hopkins and Wylie Funeral Home done lost my mama."

The McClain family stayed calm and continued their viewing, forgiving the error we'd made with the clothing and the casket. The Braxton family was out of the whole mess and thoroughly pleased and enjoying their family hour. But with the Johnson family in complete turmoil, Mr. Wylie was still on the line with Johns Hopkins. They finally told him that the only other woman released on that day was a white woman, so that ruled out the theory that something had gone wrong at the hospital. Neither Ms. Johnson nor Ms. McClain was still wearing a toe tag, so it was difficult to retrace what had happened.

A few minutes later Ms. Johnson's daughter returned to the door with the police. There was nothing they could do at that point; a crime hadn't been committed. Mr. Wylie called Ms. Johnson's son into his office and allowed him to speak with the hospital. About an hour later Ms. Johnson's other daughter showed up and asked to speak with Mr. Wylie.

"Wylie, what's going on? I want to see my mother."

He explained to her what had happened, but she still insisted on seeing the body. She walked up to the casket and inspected the woman we'd thought a couple of hours before was Ms. McClain.

"That's Mama. Yup, that's my mother. That's her mole right there. Wylie, this is my mother."

Mr. Wylie looked stunned.

"You look like you got shit on your face," she told him.

We never figured out how it happened, but Ms. McClain and Ms. Johnson had gotten mixed up in the basement before their bodies were fully prepared and had ended up in the wrong clothes and caskets. Ms. Johnson's starlet daughter did not even show up to the service the next day. I'm not sure if it was the shame of not recognizing her mother or if it was disgust at the mix-up.

We got only one chance at funeral service, as Mr. Wylie never let us forget. For the first time in eight years, we'd blown it.

• • • •

THE seasons were changing. Flip-flops were no longer acceptable, and thin cardigans were exchanged for heavy parkas. The air was stale, trees half-naked, ground lukewarm, skies kind of cloudy. October had proven to be one of our busiest months. Ranked third behind January and February, October normally finished with about thirty calls. Maybe it was the shift in the weather, or maybe it was easier for pneumonia to settle into the lungs of cancer and AIDS patients. Maybe the spirits began recruiting early for All Hallows' Eve. Whatever the reason, for thirty-one days, we were slaves for the dead.

Every hand was occupied and every hour of the workday was accounted for. Five death calls had come in over the weekend, which left me swamped. I couldn't find a clean space on my desk that morning. Piles of case folders were stacked high as the calls rolled in, and while I still needed to close out the cases from the previous month, new death certificates and pieces of paper with the names and phone numbers of doctors who needed to sign them were scattered all around. As usual, I would have to sort through the whirlwind of paper and make sense of it all. It was early in the morning and I knew my long day of sorting, filing, and straining my eyes to decode Wylie's shorthand had only just begun.

The elder Wylie had been sitting at my desk the night before as the ashes and butts in the ashtray there proved. I kept asking him not to leave his ashtray on my desk, but it was always late when he came back at night to follow up on cases and smoke, and the last thing he was going to do was think about cleaning up to please me.

Before I could transfer the phone lines back over from the answering service, Mr. Wylie was already calling on the free line to make sure that I'd arrived at work on time. Always, he had a list of instructions at the ready to give me.

"Morning," he started in his pre-coffee voice. It was heavy and dry, like an older, raspy version of himself.

"Good morning," I said in my "You know I'm not a morning person" voice. It took me a few minutes to warm up when I first arrived in the morning, but Mr. Wylie usually understood that.

"I have an eleven and a twelve o'clock."

"Here? Or Liberty Road?"

"Liberty Road at eleven. I'll be there at twelve. The doctor's name should be on your desk. Call and see what time we can pick up the death certificate."

"Done." I scribbled a few notes as he was talking.

Pause. Silence. He was thinking.

"I already made arrangements for Jones. The folder should be on your desk."

"I don't see it."

"Well, look in my briefcase."

"Got it."

"'ey. How you?" He wasn't talking to me this time. He never said "hold on."

"Uh, hello . . ." I was talking in vain. I put the phone on speaker and went on to something else. After a few minutes he returned to the conversation.

"I still have two bodies out. One is at the medical examiner's, the other at Sinai Hospital. Call and see if they are ready. I want everybody in the house."

"Yes, sir! We'll get everyone in the house."

"What about my money?"

"What about it?"

"Do we need to go to the bank this morning?"

"I have two insurance checks and cash in my drawer."

"Send Kevin to the bank."

"I will."

"Talk to ya."

Our conversations had become short and awkward after Mr. Wylie discovered that Brandon and I had been together. We never spoke directly about it, but I almost felt as though Mr. Wylie thought I'd committed some kind of incestuous act behind his back. I was his little girl and Brandon was his little boy, and I don't think he ever imagined us together.

CHAPTER
FIFTEEN

ON a Friday morning, the day after autumn had become official, it still felt like summer. The sun was shining brighter than it ever had, and the open windows let in a bare breeze. But within minutes, that Friday at the end of September became the coldest day of my existence.

Each day at five o'clock exactly I would turn off the part of my brain that thought about funerals, death, and the Wylies. That rule kept me sane after my falling out with Brandon. But for some reason, late Monday night earlier that week, I'd suddenly remembered that I had forgotten to cancel our organist and minister for a service the next day. The family had changed their mind at the last minute and decided to go with their own choice.

Mr. Wylie was going to be furious, but I picked up the phone and called him anyway. He wasn't upset at all, much to my surprise. He told me we would just inform Pastor Bates and

SHERI BOOKER

Mr. Bufford in the morning and would give them a check for
their inconvenience.

The next morning, Pastor Bates arrived bright and early for
his check, but our organist, Mr. Bufford, didn't show up at all. It
was out of character for him to turn down money, but when he
didn't come I assumed Mr. Wylie had talked to him and they'd
figured out another way to compensate him for the mix-up.

It was a slow week and no one needed an organist, so none
of us called Mr. Bufford in the days that followed. Then on
Friday morning, I got a call from his best friend while I was in
the middle of reading my entertainment gossip. His friend
hadn't heard from him all week either, which we both thought
was strange. I wished him luck tracking Mr. Bufford down, but
for some reason, my mind started wandering. Monday was the
last time his best friend had spoken to him and it was also the
day that I had forgotten to call him. It started to feel like a bizarre coincidence. So I called Mr. Wylie to see if he had talked
to Mr. Bufford at all in the last few days. He hadn't either.

That afternoon Mr. Wylie and I were headed out to look
at a funeral home for sale in Northwest Baltimore. An older
director needed a buyer because his license had been revoked.
He'd become senile, and on a few occasions he had forgotten
to properly inter his bodies. A few had decomposed in the
basement and one of the affected families had reported him to
the state board, which had resulted in a lawsuit.

Bufford's house was on the way to the funeral home, so I
asked Mr. Wylie to stop by. He thought I was being ridiculous.
Bufford was probably at home relaxing, he suspected. When
we arrived at his home, Bufford's gold Lexus with "Stan" in
bold letters on the license plate was not there. I convinced Mr.

Wylie to go knock on the door, and when he went up on the porch the storm door was locked. There was a few days' worth of mail piled up in the screen.

We decided that he was probably out of town, which didn't seem too far-fetched, since he played in a church on Sundays in New York. But while we'd been out running errands, Buford's brother had come to the funeral home looking for him too. When we got back, I called the friend I'd talked to in the morning to get the name of the church Mr. Bufford played for in New York. But the pastor there hadn't seen any sign of Bufford. As we spoke, I started panicking. He could have just taken a trip somewhere else, I knew, but I couldn't help worrying that he'd been abducted or carjacked or in a terrible accident. It just seemed too ominous that the people closest to him had no clue where he was. With the worst-case scenario playing over and over in my head, I started bugging Mr. Wylie to file a police report. Mr. Wylie still thought I was nuts.

After what felt like hours of what Mr. Wylie called "foolishness," I got back to work. It was almost time for my three o'clock appointment with the family of a cousin of Mr. Wylie's. They were coming in to prearrange a funeral. People normally prearranged to make sure that they had enough money saved down the line. Midway through our meeting, I was interrupted by the intercom.

"Bufford in the house dead!" Mr. Wylie yelled.

My heart felt like it stopped beating. I temporarily went deaf and couldn't make out the words Mr. Wylie's cousin was saying to me. I excused myself and ran upstairs to Mr. Wylie. He looked dumbfounded; he and Bufford had gone to high school together. Was he sure? But Mr. Wylie had talked to

Bufford's brother and found out Bufford had been dead for four days inside his own home. Blunt force trauma to his head. No sign of his car. They definitely knew it was him because his fingers were in perfect condition. Dead.

His brother was the one who found him in the end. After missing us at the funeral home, he called the police and they went to his house and knocked the glass out of a window to find a horrific scene. There were splotches of blood smeared across the living room leading into the basement; Bufford lay on the basement steps. The decomposition combined with the brutal shots he'd taken to his head made him unrecognizable.

I couldn't help thinking that maybe if I had called him that Monday night to tell him about the schedule change, he would still be alive. The sound of his phone ringing might have stopped the hands that had turned against him.

Mr. Wylie called me Saturday afternoon and told us the family had chosen us to render the services.

When I arrived at work on Monday morning, Bufford wasn't there yet, but Mr. Wylie was sitting out on the stoop when I pulled up. He'd sent Kevin to pick up Bufford's body and we all walked into the building together when he returned. Mr. Wylie warned us about what we were about to see. He'd seen the body the day before at the coroner's. When he unzipped the body bag, I was stunned to see the foreign object before me. This was not the man I spoke to several times a week, the man who sang people out of their seats. He looked nothing like himself, and the dazzling jaw that he could magically manipulate while he sang was now hanging ajar limply. He was five shades darker than he'd been when he was alive, and his skin had started to deteriorate. It looked like a layer had slipped off, and you could see where the decomposition had set in. There were gashes in his face where his skin was still in place and holes in the back of his head. It was horrifying. We quickly zipped the bag back up and I went upstairs to my office feeling completely numb. It didn't seem real.

As the day passed, I sat at my desk still in a daze. I neglected my daily ritual of reading headlines and blogs. Kevin came upstairs and handed me Bufford's death certificate. It was official. The medical examiner had ruled his death a homicide. As soon as I un-forwarded the phone lines from our answering service, they began ringing off the hook.

"Do you have Stan's body? When is Bufford's funeral?"

I had no answers.

We had other cases that week, but most of our attention was on Bufford. When I printed out his picture for the marquee downstairs, Tuverla walked in and took the photo from Kevin.

"Tell me who did this. Tell me who did this," she said while shaking her head. Mr. Wylie hadn't sat still since it happened.

Mr. Bufford had to have a closed casket. Though when it came to restoring a corpse Mr. Wylie was a magician, he wouldn't be able to revive his friend. The decomposition was just too bad. That day with all of us in the basement was the last time he would be viewed. His family chose a white and gold casket with musical notes on the corners for him, and Mr. Wylie had it engraved with his name across the top. The funeral was on a Saturday morning. Since there wasn't a viewing, his friends had a musical tribute for him the night before. I was so distraught I wasn't sure I could take sitting through the services, but I knew I owed it to him to be there. The church was packed from the front door to the back, but I was able to find a seat in the balcony with a friend. It felt like we were at the service of a dignitary. There were more than ten preachers in robes gathered around the pulpit and a combined choir. The obituary listed five different choirs that would sing during the funeral the next day.

We sat there and looked down at the closed casket. To our surprise, after all of the phone calls and inquiries, only six floral arrangements were sent to the church for the service. I surveyed the sanctuary and couldn't shake the feeling that Bufford's killer was there. I poked my friend every time I saw someone suspicious. There was a boy sitting in front us with a fresh scratch on his face. What if that was him? My mind was going crazy. Plus it had been a while since I'd actually attended a funeral, so it was hard for me to sit still.

We sat there listening to all the kind speeches about Bufford, and then the choir began to sing "Precious Lord, Take My Hand," and my friend began crying. I smacked her hand because crying was definitely against the rules.

• • • •

THEY say death comes in threes, and I was starting to believe it. My stomach sank when Mr. Wylie called for his morning check-in a few days before Thanksgiving and said, "Call Maryland General and see if Rodney Britt is ready."

He already knew that I would be devastated by the news. Rodney was the brother of my dear friend Michael.

"When did it happen?"

"This morning."

"I'll call you—" I couldn't finish my sentence.

I had to call my friend Michael, but I had no clue what I would say. Strangely, working so close to death hadn't made knowing that the right words give people comfort any easier. I hated when I heard someone at our services say "God knew what he was doing" or "She's in a better place now." It felt so empty.

I called Michael from my cell phone and simply said, "Whatever you need, I am here. I am here, whatever you need." I didn't want to say anything else. I didn't know if God made the right call or if his brother was actually in a better place. The only thing I knew for sure was that as long as we had the body, his brother wouldn't have to worry about a thing.

The call was going to the Liberty Road facility, meaning that Brandon would handle the arrangements. I sat at the desk pondering what to do next. I wanted the best for Rodney, but Brandon and I were still on the outs, so I knew talking with him about the preparations would be awkward. I started thinking of all of our exclusive amenities, like the sixteen-by-twenty-inch memory portrait and the set of personalized bookmarks we gave to special families. This family was special.

In the end, we were all in agreement about this case—the Britts were an important family in the community. That night we all gathered to work the busy viewing, which brought in distinguished visitors, including the mayor of Baltimore City. Mr. Wylie even hired a harpist to play in the outside corridor, and flowers lined the chapel from wall to wall.

The next morning, I arrived at the church in an all-cream ensemble with a matching cream and gold overcoat. I plucked out the curls in my hair and layered blush on my foundation for a flawless finish. My lips were well glossed. Whenever one of us knew a family personally, we showboated a bit and took credit for the arrangements. I fell in sync with the rest of the Wylie clan, who were there directing the funeral. I was there to be seen by the movers and shakers.

After a few hours of songs and words of comfort, we were preparing to go to the cemetery. The funeral procession was ridiculously long, mainly because the guests could not wait to get to the repast; Mr. Timmy's catering company had spread an extravagant feast of crab cakes and stuffed chicken breast.

The Britts had chosen an exclusive new section of the cemetery for Rodney where there were only five other plots at the time. As I walked back toward Mr. Wylie's car after the ceremony, he told me before he pulled off that I was to ride with Brandon. I was content with ignoring this command and asked Kevin if I could ride back with him in the flower car, but Brandon grabbed me and said, "Mr. Wylie said you have to ride with me."

It had been more than six months since Brandon and I had had a real conversation. Instead, we usually sent messages through his secretary. Gone were the days when we'd enjoyed handling so much of the business together. We'd once tag-teamed Mr. Wylie with ideas for marketing and public relations, but now I was purposely disagreeing with all of Brandon's ideas.

In the car to the repast hall, we sat in silence. Finally he asked why I wasn't talking to him.

"Duh. Like you don't know."

"What? Are you mad at me or something?"

We were back to stony silence.

"I don't hate you," I said. "I just don't like what you did."

"I'm sorry. I know I was wrong."

"I miss you."

"I miss you too."

I accepted his apology and buried my grudge, at least as much as I could. If anyone knew that life was too short to hold a grudge, it was the two of us.

• • • •

ALTHOUGH Brandon and I were learning to be civil to each other again, things between Mr. Wylie and me were changing.

The year had been quite difficult for the business. The new funeral home had not caught on the way we'd all expected it to. Old habits die hard, and the people in Baltimore County still seemed to want to go to the city to make funeral arrangements. We had lost Bufford and we hadn't fully recovered from Billy's sudden death. Handling the cases of people so near and dear to us was starting to take a toll on me. I couldn't stay numb anymore. And even though it was an ambiguous loss, losing Ms. Angela left the biggest void. Even with all my experience, I couldn't hold things together like she did. And the office had become tense. For the first time in Wylie history, Mr. Wylie was swearing. "This is my shithouse," he would say when he wanted to remind us that he was still in charge. Or when a family or one of our vendors was trying to pull a fast one on him, he would say "Shucks," in a long, drawn-out way. We hardly agreed on anything anymore, and our short conversations were getting ever shorter.

Even so, I followed in Ms. Angela's footsteps and never took off from work, even when I was sick. One morning, I went to work with a toothache and got a call from a client named Darren, who was inquiring about funeral prices for his mother. I talked him through what we offered and we scheduled an appointment time for him to come in and make the arrangements. After meeting with Mr. Wylie in the afternoon, he still felt the need to shop around to a few other funeral homes before he decided whom to entrust with his mother. That should have been my first tip-off that he was going to be difficult.

By the next morning, he had decided to go with us, and he and a tribe of family members invaded our arrangement area. There were so many of them that they couldn't all fit inside the four-by-four-foot room. As usual, I sat with the family and recorded the basic information we needed. Darren was so distraught that he kept mixing up the important details, which made a mess out of the card. I knew I would have to make corrections before Mr. Wylie saw it.

The following day Darren called the office and asked to speak to Mr. Wylie. "He's not available. Can I help you with something?" I asked.

"I needed to talk to him about my mother," he said.

I recognized his voice. "Hi, Darren. This is Sheri. What did you need?"

"I need to give him the insurance policy number."

"Okay, great. I was waiting on you to call yesterday. What's the number, sweetie?"

There was a pause, and then he said angrily, "You know what? I don't want to talk to you. Where is Mr. Wylie? You're gonna make me come down there and smack the taste out of your mouth." *Click.* He hung up.

I couldn't believe the attitude I'd just gotten, but I also

knew that during what was often one of the worst times of their lives, people said things and acted in ways that were out of character. It had certainly happened before. But it was the first time in Wylie history that I had ever been actually threatened, or hung up on so abruptly for that matter. I called Mr. Wylie to tell him about Darren's threat and strategize about what we would do next. I figured we would have a laugh about it, although I was still shaky with shock. While I was still on the line with Mr. Wylie, Darren called on our other line, so I placed Mr. Wylie on hold.

"Did you call him yet?" Darren said immediately, with no greeting.

"No." I lied because I wasn't sure when Mr. Wylie would call him back.

"I'm on my way there, and you better not be there when I get there." *Click.* He had threatened and hung up on me again. Now I was furious.

I clicked over to Mr. Wylie. "He threatened me again."

"What did he say?"

I told him and he asked for Darren's phone number.

Mr. Wylie hung up with me and called Darren. It was about five minutes before he called me back.

"I just talked to the boy. You shouldn't have told him that you were waiting for him to call."

"Huh?"

"And he said you called him sweetie."

"I just said, 'What's the number, sweetie.' No big deal."

"You have to be more sensitive to people like him."

"People like who? You mean people that threaten people?"

"You know, people like him." We all had assumed that

Darren was gay because of his mannerisms. "They already dis-
like women. You just can't say stuff like that." His voice was
firm.

"So you think it's okay for him to threaten me?"

I couldn't control myself. In a flash my finger hit the switch
hook and Mr. Wylie and I were no longer connected. The
phone rang two seconds later.

"Did you hang up on me?"

"Yes. I have a toothache and I'm not in the mood to argue."

We got off the phone. I was pissed that Mr. Wylie had allowed Darren to talk to me like he had and had even acted as
if it was my fault for provoking him. It was the first time Mr.
Wylie hadn't taken my side.

The same day a woman called me and asked if the death
certificate for her mother's boyfriend was ready. I explained
that it was not ready and that I'd call her as soon as it came in.
It was sitting on my desk and had not been filed at Vital Records yet. Since I was the only one there and everyone else was
out on a service, there was no way to get the death certificate
authenticated, and so I knew she wouldn't get it until at least
the following Monday morning.

After she hung up with me, the woman immediately called
Mr. Wylie's cell phone to complain that she wasn't going to get
the death certificate fast enough. Five minutes later he was
standing in front of me.

"Do you need to go home for the rest of the day?"

"Excuse me?" I asked.

"I mean since your tooth is aching. Do you need to take
the rest of the day off?"

"No. I'm fine."

"Well, you can't be fine if two people have made complaints against you."

Two complaints in one day seemed to outweigh the zero complaints in eight years. I couldn't believe that he was questioning my authority with our clients. I shut down my computer, grabbed my cell phone, and stormed out the door. I was tired of being abused by grieving families who didn't remember their harsh words or threats the next day. As I unlocked my car door, years of tears began pouring. I hadn't cried since Patricia's son's viewing, and it felt like such an enormous relief to finally let it all out—tears that I had been holding on to for years for the suicide victim, and the baby I dressed, Billy, Bufford, Ms. Angela, and Brandon.

I sat in my car and thought about all the families that I had helped over the years. I was always the one who had to carry the messages between Mr. Wylie and the families. I always had to be the bigger person, the understanding one, no matter what was thrown my way. But I didn't want to be strong or polite anymore.

The next afternoon Mr. Wylie called and asked if I could meet him at the funeral home, and he was sitting at my desk lighting a cigarette when I walked in. I sat down in the chair across from him, feeling a strong sense that I didn't want to be there. We both seemed to understand the end was nearing.

"How's your tooth?"

"It still hurts."

We sat in silence for a while, and then he began talking. "When I get two complaints about you in one day, I have to bring it to your attention."

"I agree."

He asked me to come in on Monday morning to help him finish up his cases. I agreed and we were back on the same page, at least for a while.

But after the Darren incident, for the first time ever, working at the funeral home felt like real work. I could feel my status with Mr. Wylie slowly diminishing. He was giving more responsibility to Tuverla and passing off my projects to the office manager at Liberty Road. I didn't like it one bit.

But I would never have quit on him, even though I had reached my ceiling years before. If I didn't plan on going to mortuary school, there was nowhere left for me to go. I was already basically running Gilmor Street, and Wylie certainly wasn't going to pay me more to do what I was already doing. I was fine with that because it had never been about money. I stayed because of the loyalty we had for each other. But now that was gone too.

EPILOGUE

STRETCHED out on a private beach in Montego Bay, I melted under the Caribbean sun. Its warmth reminded me that I was still very much alive. I shielded my eyes behind a pair of oversize sunglasses, not only to block the rays, but also to hide the tears that were falling uncontrollably. Something about that beach made me feel closer to God. Maybe it was the way the waves crashed against the sand or the harmony of the birds around me. It was as though the universe was telling me there was more beyond the small part of the world I'd been living in. And more than anything I wanted to feel that fullness again.

I was no longer ashamed to cry. Every time I had held my tears back over the years, I had become a little less human, a little less compassionate. I had already died a hundred deaths during my time working at Wylie Funeral Home, and now it was time to live the only life I'd get. Each time we buried someone, a small piece of me was gnawed away, until eventually I felt almost nothing. I lived with people's stories. I was left with their secrets. Imagine having hundreds of obituaries catalogued in your brain, bits and pieces of unsolved homicides, and real faces programmed into your memory: the innocent children, the sweet old ladies, the handsome men, all gone too soon.

I spent the afternoons of my vacation sitting in an Internet café posting my résumé on Monster.com: I was now a twenty-four-year-old unemployed woman. One thing was certain: When I returned home in a few days I would have to find a way to reincarnate myself.

. . . .

I had walked away from Wylie Funeral Home with everything that belonged to me, except my last paycheck, stuffed into two bags. I knew that I would never be going back there, at least not while I was still breathing.

The way I was feeling, I wanted to wipe out Mr. Wylie's whole computer, delete all the case files and the spreadsheets that calculated our revenue and outstanding balances. I wanted to erase any trace of my existence at that place. He had done the same thing to Ms. Angela. Why did I believe that I was exempt from his mercurial streak? Why did I think I was special and that he wouldn't kick me out like all the others?

I'd known it was coming when I walked into work one morning and found that my vacation request had been denied. I had followed protocol for getting days off to go to a friend's wedding in Jamaica, posting my request on the bulletin board about three or four weeks before my trip. It was nothing fancy, just a printout that read "Sheri out of the office June 15–19." That's how we always did it. I asked for only three days off, which didn't seem like much in the grand scheme of things.

Then about a week before my trip, I came into the office and found my request sheet ripped from the board and thrown on my desk. There was a line drawn through the dates of the trip and the words "No Way" scribbled at the bottom. I knew that it was Mr. Wylie's doing. A little after two, he strode into the office dressed in one of his impeccable black suits after finishing his second service of the day. Earlier that morning he'd dropped into one of Brandon's funerals and then met Tuverla at the cemetery to close out her service. With Brandon and Tuverla directing funerals and me handling the business aspects at Gilmor Street, Mr. Wylie had a little more freedom but still not a lot of time. So I had to catch him when I could.

Even though I had a list of business items I needed to discuss with him, I was focused only on the disrespectful way he was acting. I'd seen his attitude a million times before, but he'd never pulled it out that way with me, and I wasn't having it.

I waited to bring it up until he went into the kitchen, which had always been neutral ground. No one had ever been fired or subjected to Mr. Wylie's scolding there. I sat down across from him while he ate a cheesesteak sub.

"Ericka's graduation is on Saturday. I have your ticket." He spoke first, reminding me of his stepdaughter's ceremony.

"I'm so proud of her. Who else is coming?" I smiled, relieved that we had something lighthearted to talk about to break the ice.

"Brandon, Charleen, and her godmother," he answered quickly.

I had never missed a Wylie family function, and Ericka was like a little sister to me. The tickets were limited and so I was honored to be included. It was the perfect time for me to segue into talking about my vacation, so I went for it.

"So . . . you know I won't be here on June fifteenth to nineteenth," I said in the same conversational manner we had already established.

"Yes, you will," he said between chews, in one of his signature ambiguous tones that left you wondering if he was serious about what you'd just heard. The urn for "employees past" sat between us on the table, but I continued to speak up anyway.

"I will actually be out of the country." I softened my voice even more.

He took one of his long pauses.

"Well, if you go, that's it!" He sounded definitive, as if he was giving me an ultimatum.

"That's fine," I said, throwing him attitude right back.

He sat there eating his lunch while I went back into my office to finish my work. I was fuming. I wasn't asking for his permission. I was paying him a courtesy.

On Saturday morning I showed up for Ericka's graduation. Mr. Wylie had saved me a seat with his family in the huge cathedral, and afterward we posed for pictures like a big happy family. Brandon had to leave to go make funeral arrangements, but the rest of us went to brunch after the ceremony. Mr. Wylie was in his element, and I thought for sure he had come to his senses.

The week went by rapidly, and before I knew it, the day I

was scheduled to leave for Jamaica had arrived. Knowing I had a busy day ahead of me, I rushed in to work to get started on my cases so I wouldn't leave any loose ends. I walked into Wylie Funeral Home just like it was any other day, propping the two wooden doors open in the vestibule as I came in and sliding the sign from "Call" to "Please ring the bell." The alarm was still on, which meant that I was the first person to arrive.

Mr. Wylie didn't call until about two thirty in the afternoon. When I picked up the phone, I was standing by the desk near the kitchen.

"So what time will you be here tomorrow?" Mr. Wylie led the conversation by saying.

I laughed nervously. "Come on, Mr. Wylie. You know I really won't be here. What's the big deal? I never ask for vacation time. Everything is covered. Why won't you let me go?"

He paused. "So you mean to tell me that you won't be here Thursday, Friday, or Monday, but you come back on Tuesday."

"Yes," I interjected. "It's just three little days."

He was thinking.

"Since you think that, you can leave my keys when you're done for the day."

In two seconds he had stolen nine years from me.

I held myself together long enough to respond to him.

"No problem," I called out to him before slamming the receiver down. My entire body was flushed with fire, and I could hardly breathe. I couldn't believe that he had cut me loose so swiftly over the phone. I deserved more from him. But though I could have called back and begged him to reconsider, I just didn't have the will to fight.

I didn't say a word to anyone that afternoon. I just quietly assembled my belongings. Piece by piece, memory by memory, file by file. Nine years stuffed into two bags.

• • • •

WHEN I returned from Jamaica, I hit a wall of withdrawal. I wondered if Mr. Wylie remembered that we had an appointment to make prearrangements scheduled for that Saturday, or if he knew I had five thousand dollars in cash stashed away in a folder in my drawer because I hadn't had time to make it to the bank. There was a lot of unfinished business, and it hurt to even think about it. To keep my mind off things, I headed to Los Angeles for a few weeks. While I was there, one of my friends from graduate school called and offered me the opportunity to spend the next year as an editorial assistant at her literary magazine in South Africa. For the first time I started to believe that maybe Mr. Wylie had done me a favor by letting me go. I'd traveled outside of Baltimore more than ever before in the last few weeks, and unbelievably, going to Africa was now a real possibility for me.

Now that I could look forward to a new adventure, I decided to e-mail Mr. Wylie with all the loose ends. In my note, I thanked him for opening up his business to me nine years ago and for teaching me so much. I told him that I loved him and we were both Christians so we couldn't act this way. I wished him the best with the business, and then I told him I would be spending the next year in South Africa. Putting it in writing made it feel official.

I didn't think he would write me back, but he did. He told

me that he had told his wife a year ago that it was time for me to move on. And maybe we both just got too comfortable. He was happy that I was going to South Africa. He would miss me. He signed it "Your friend always."

That October, I was in New York City meeting with a publisher when my phone rang. It was Mr. Wylie. I sent the call straight to voice mail. A few seconds later my phone was vibrating again; it was Brandon. I also sent him to voice mail. Then I started to panic. *Who died?* I thought. That was the only reason I could imagine the two of them calling me. I excused myself from the room and dialed Mr. Wylie back.

"Sheri!" he said in that unmistakable booming voice.

"Yes, Mr. Wylie?" I responded impatiently as if I were busy.

"Everybody be quiet. I got Sheri on the phone," he hushed the voices in the background.

"How can I help you?" I asked, preparing for some horrible news.

But then he said, "Where do we order the burgundy folders from?"

"Uh, probably a company that makes folders, a printing company, someone who binds paper. How would I know?" I couldn't believe this was why he was calling me, but I was so relieved that no one had died.

"Don't you get smart with me," he said in the tone we usually joked in.

"Don't call me asking about burgundy folders," I snapped back. "Don't play with me." We both laughed.

"You know what? I actually need access to the funeral home for my book." I needed to review a few files for research.

"You are always welcome here. You still have your key," he said, as though he didn't remember stripping it from me that day.

"No, I don't."

"Well, I'll give it to your mother in church on Sunday."

"Okay. Crescent Sales."

"Huh?"

"Crescent Sales is the name of the company."

"Thanks."

"You're welcome," I replied, and couldn't help but grin.

• • • •

WHEN you spend almost a decade working in funeral service, there are some things you learn to forget. Tears were the first thing I sacrificed to become a part of the business. But I mistook control over my tears for control over myself.

As I reached deep down to find the words to tell this story, I found the residue of emotions that I had buried within myself, feelings that I couldn't articulate at the time, memories that I camouflaged in the spongiest parts of my brain. And now that I'm older, they resurface.

"I see dead people." No, that's not just some line from a Bruce Willis movie; it's the testament of my life. Some faces, no matter how deeply caked with mortuary makeup, are unforgettable. Take, for instance, the brown wrinkly skin of the little old lady from the nursing home a few blocks away from the funeral home. I don't remember her name, but I still see her face. I studied it one night before we closed, amazed by how deep the indented lines sank into her face. They looked like a maze. I ran my fingers across them one by one.

She was laid out in a blue dinghy, the cheap felt-covered box that poor folks were buried in. I sat upstairs for four hours in my good church clothes, waiting to escort people in to see her, but not one person came to pay their respects. Where was her family? Her neighbors? Her deacon? Her best girlfriend? Had she outlived everyone? I knew living to be eightysomething was a blessing. But if that was the case, how could dying at that age be so lonely?

Yes, I see dead people. I remember some of the faces that were pushed in on gurneys, wrapped in hospital sheets, recently pierced with IVs. I remember bloated bodies. Some as stiff as a board, some rubbery, some grazed with bullet holes, some in perfect condition. I also remember the angelic faces. The woman who was just too beautiful to die. And too young to die of AIDS. She looked like Snow White or Sleeping Beauty, and I wished that someone could kiss her back to life. The medicine she had been taking before her death had made her hair so curly and shiny.

Last March, just days before my birthday, I got a call from my cousin Annie. Only three months apart, we grew up like sisters. Her voice was trembling. "Can you come sit with me?"

"Where are you?" I asked. She was sitting alone at the hospital. I thought there was something wrong with her four-year-old daughter because she suffers from sickle cell, but it wasn't Kelsey—it was Annie's husband. They'd gotten up that morning and had breakfast. He went to use the bathroom and asked her to fetch him a glass of apple juice. Before she could return with the apple juice, he was lying on the bathroom floor with his boxers still around his ankles. Now they were at the hospital. The nurses had put her in a room by herself and would not tell her anything about his condition until someone else arrived.

It was raining that morning. I jumped up and threw on some clothes. I don't know where it came from, but I started crying before I even left the house. As I walked through the doors of the emergency room, I heard the chilling screams of my cousin. I rushed back to the room and wrapped my arms around her. For once I knew being strong for her wasn't enough. She needed more. So I let my tears fall and mix with hers.

I'd always believed that death held a lesson for those left behind. But when my cousin lost her husband, who was only thirty, and became a single mother of three, I saw no lesson in it. When a seemingly healthy man, whom I had seen just the day before, drops dead while peeing, I don't see the meaning.

Death has been many things to me, but it's never been fair.

I don't regret saving my tears all those years. It was the one thing I walked away with from Wylie Funeral Home. Not a church fan, not a pen, not a paycheck. I walked away with a bank full of tears.

ACKNOWLEDGMENTS

I couldn't have told this story without the Wylie Family—Al and Brandon— who showed me how to connect life with death and how to love unconditionally. I found love in that funeral home, a second father, lifelong friends Angela Johnson (RIP), Cindy, Renisse, Tuverla, Charleen, Ericka, Hari Close, John Williams, and Cousin Lou.

To my family—Mommy, Daddy, Chantá, and my grandmother Annie—whose support helped me to close the dark chapters and begin my new life as a writer. I can never repay you for the love . . . the love . . . the love . . . the love.

To my big brother, Michael Britton, and your infinite support. And my spiritual advisor, Jamal-Harrison Bryant.

To the distinguished Goucher faculty who mentored me— Tom French (who believed in this project from its inception), Laura Wexler, Leslie Rubinkowski, and Phillip Gerard (you gave me CPR just when I was about to give up). And Patsy Sims for the awesome program that you oversee.

To my good friend and mentor, Maggie Messitt: Thanks for being like a sister, editor, confidante, all-around good girlfriend.

Chenia Leak, you were my rock through my many edits and revisions; thanks for locking me out of Twitter and Facebook so I could focus. Eleina Ouaffai-Campbell, you don't know how much you inspire me.

To my girls, Natalie Lawson, Kee Siler, Antoinette Walker, Paula Campbell, Maya Gilmore, for reading or listening or suggesting or something like that. You know the role you played in this process.

And to Leslie F. Miller, there aren't any words. I can't thank you enough. You're the best and I love you.

And to Floyd T. for saving our butts on that infamous night.

Thank you to Femi Lawal, Sir Reigns, Faye Wallace, Kenji Jasper, Tayari Jones, Felicia Pride, Jennifer Ogunsola, Heather Harris, Alex Coleman, Roger Kerson.

To the greatest literary agent, Betsy Lerner—you never panicked and we did it.

To the best editor a girl could have, Lucia Watson, thank you for your patience and dedication to this project. I am forever grateful. To Gigi Campo and the rest of the Gotham Books staff, thank you.

To Dr. Mary Beth Pope—you're the reason I write nonfiction.

To South Africa, St. Lucia, Rehoboth, Madison, Jersey, Cali, all the places that welcomed me to write. Margaret Hepp, Maureen Codd, Tracey Samuelson, Andrew Starner, and everyone else from Amazwi who lived through this with me. To the amazing SOMA students, who gave me a reason to smile each day.

To all my students, past and present (CCBC, SWAGG, Baltimore Leadership School for Young Women, Stevenson University), thank you for your understanding during this process.

And to Dr. John Nesbitt, thanks for taking such good care of my mother. I finally finished this book.

To Jasmine and Zoe Davis, Kelsey, Madison, and MacKenzie Walker, and Kay-lee Harris, I do this all for you.

There are some people who didn't make it to see this book published, but I know they are here in spirit just the same: Ms. Angela, Big Mama, Jason, Mr. Oliver, Cousin Billy, Grandma Lula, Daddy Mack.

Thank you, God. Amen!